CHARLES PEACE

THE
MASTER CRIMINAL

THE LIFE STORY OF CHARLES PEACE

ILLUSTRATED

**Fredonia Books
Amsterdam, The Netherlands**

The Master Criminal:
The Life Story of Charles Peace

by
Anonymous

ISBN: 1-4101-0459-1

Copyright © 2004 by Fredonia Books

Reprinted from the 1911 edition

Fredonia Books
Amsterdam, The Netherlands
http://www.fredoniabooks.com

All rights reserved, including the right to reproduce this book, or portions thereof, in any form.

In order to make original editions of historical works available to scholars at an economical price, this facsimile of the original edition of 1911 is reproduced from the best available copy and has been digitally enhanced to improve legibility, but the text remains unaltered to retain historical authenticity.

CONTENTS

CHAPTER		PAGE
	Introduction	9
I.	Peace Makes His Entrance upon Life's Stage	10
II.	Early Crimes	16
III.	First Term of Penal Servitude	20
IV.	Peace the Convict	25
V.	The Death of Sims	29
VI.	The Shadow of the Gallows	35
VII.	The Murder of Mr. Dyson	39
VIII.	The Murder Hunt Commences	43
IX.	Peace the Wanderer	47
X.	The Meeting with the Traitress Sue	50
XI.	The Home at Peckham	54
XII.	A Burglary or So	61
XIII.	A Few More Burglaries	68
XIV.	Peace the Jester	75
XV.	Peace Meets an Imitator	79
XVI.	The Arrest of P. C. Robinson	82
XVII.	Peace Stories told after the Arrest	85
XVIII.	Peace: Possibilities and Might-have-beens	92
XIX.	Ex-detective Parrock Speaks	96
XX.	What the Police and the Newspapers Did	101
XXI.	Peace's Last Adventure	107
XXII.	The Great Trial	115
XXIII.	Peace's Last Days	120
XXIV.	The Execution	125
	Conclusion	127

LIST OF ILLUSTRATIONS

	PAGE
Portrait of Charles Peace.........................*Frontispiece*	
On the top of the wall Peace and his deadly enemy closed for combat	31
He invited the constable into the stable	56
Standing in the doorway was the huge towering form of the butler	63
Out shot the burglar's fist	71
"Here, guv'nor, hold that for me"	94
Peace had to be literally forced into the compartment	108
Peace sentenced to death	119

THE MASTER CRIMINAL

THE LIFE STORY OF CHARLES PEACE
INTRODUCTION

Down in the depths of London's Chamber of Horrors stands the waxen image of a man.

To reach it you must descend a flight of steps flanked by massive blocks of stone like the walls of a prison.

You must run the gauntlet of groups of staring figures, silent enough but horribly eloquent in their repulsiveness. You must pass scores of hideous object-lessons in human depravity.

And yet the figure we have come in search of in this gruesome place is that of a genius—perverted perhaps—but still, for all that, the effigy of a man who, but for a certain indescribable something, might have risen to be a leading actor, or an equally celebrated musician, or even—who knows?—a brilliant statesman.

We come upon it at last, standing by itself there in the darkest corner as though too evil even for the company of lesser murderers. Probably the first things you notice about it are the eminently respectable frock-coat and trousers with which the little old fellow is draped.

Then as your eyes become more accustomed to the gloom you take careful stock of the face. It is one that compels you to do so.

A diminutive, hunched-up man, clean shaven. Two gleaming eyes that go far back into the head so that they can watch unseen, the eyes of a hawk. A huge slit of a mouth with cruel thin lips. Jaws that look as if they were hinged on steel. Ears made for detecting the slightest sound.

Intellect? Yes, any amount of it, as evidence the lofty bulging forehead indicative of capacity for inventive thought.

Here is a man, you say, who might have been a great architect, engineer, or politician, but——

While the little old man with the prematurely white hair and the eyebrows that run strangely up to the crown of the head gazes at you from his solitary corner you take up your catalogue and read:

261. *Charles Peace, the murderer and burglar, in the character of Mr. Thompson. * * He was a bad-mad or mad-bad, and from other points of view the earth was well rid of him."*

So says the chronicler. But was he right? Or are we indeed looking upon the face of a genius whose brain has been warped by some hidden pressure of the skull, little enough known nowadays, totally undreamed of in the seventies, when Charles Peace lived and moved and had his being?

In another part of the chamber we come upon the man again. He has climbed to the heights of ignomy. Instead of the frock-coat are the prison clothes and the broad arrow. The executioner stands ready at his back. At his feet the grave is yawning for his body.

Instinctively we look for signs of craven terror on the waxen countenance but there are none. Even in this awful moment the face is calmly alert. He is smiling. Evidently he was no coward.

What was this human riddle then? What were his faults and what his virtues? Or had he any virtues at all?

Let us try to discover. We have heard of him often enough. Such as he is at last we will try to make his true acquaintance.

CHAPTER I.

Peace Makes His Entrance Upon Life's Stage.

Charles Peace made his boy to the world in general and a couple of rough if not actually criminal parents in particular in Angel Court, Sheffield, where he was born on the 14th of May, 1832.

His father was originally a tamer of wild animals but he never troubled to tame his son in whom lay concealed more than a trace of the spirit of the panther.

Almost from the first moment of the boy's sojourn on this earth his nature was given over to the things that made for wild animal excitement.

As soon as he could toddle he was out in the gutter playing with other muddy-faced mites.

By the time he was twelve the wild animal in him was already so strong that his playfellows recognised it and instinctively bowed down to his authority.

He was their self-constituted leader by right of boldness, daring, and cunning alike. He was the captain of the Angel Court gang.

Thus already, at a single spurt as it were, the babe of yesterday has flung himself into the whirlpool of early criminality. The mad race of a vicious life has already commenced.

Whether the child's early waywardness was altogether the result of inherent and incorrigible criminality, or whether it was in great part due to want of care on the part of his parents, it would be difficult to say. That it began to show itself markedly at a very early age in Charles Peace's life, the following story of his childhood will show:—

One day the boy Charles was sent by his mother to fetch beer from the neighbouring public-house. As he was walking along the street, jug in hand, a lanky youth of nearly twice his height ran up against him, sent him over on his back, breaking the jug to atoms, and then set about robbing his prey of the money he felt sure would be secreted in the boy's pockets.

But the lanky youth had mistaken his man, or boy rather. Up sprang Charles Peace, blue in the face with wrath.

"You'd take my money, would you?"

"Smack! Whack!"

The irate youngster had turned on his aggressor in a twinkling. Hot and sharp was the fight that ensued, but in the end the lanky youth, to his infinite surprise, found himself stretched flat on the pavement, with Peace standing grinning above him.

"Well," said the victor, "do you want any more?"

"No fear."

Charles Peace helped the other to his feet. "What's your name?" he asked the lanky youth.

"Dunno! They calls me Shanks, so I suppose that's good enough anyway."

"Look here, I'm captain of the Angel Court gang. I'm glad I've come up against you. I've been thinking out a little job I'd have brought off before now only it wants a pal, and there isn't a chap in my gang with nerve enough to be trusted on it."

Peace linked arms with the urchin who but five short minutes ago had tried to rob him, and began to explain himself in a scarcely audible undertone. It was characteristic of the man in his later years as well as of the boy.

In some subtle way he had divined instinctively that whereas not one of his Angel Court companions could be trusted to take their part in the crime he was proposing, this sneak thief was the very person he had been looking for for weeks past. We see the sequel to this queer alliance on the afternoon of the very next day.

A well-dressed old gentleman was walking along a quiet street leading to a well-to-do residential suburb of the town.

As he rounded a corner a strange and pathetic sight met his gaze. Lying full length, a ragged coat covering most of the face as well as the upper part of the body, was the figure of a street urchin of perhaps twelve or thirteen years of age.

Kneeling by his side was another boy, considerably bigger and older-looking, and, curiously enough, showing a very distinct and obtrusive black eye.

As the old gentleman approached the older boy bent down and addressed his prostrate companion in tones of wild despair.

"Bill, my poor old Bill, don't you know me?" Aren't you a'going to speak to me no more?"

Then, suddenly glancing up and seeing the newcomer, he ran to him with white, haggard face.

"Oh, please, sir, do come and look at my little brother Bill.

He's had an accident, sir; I know he has, though I can't say what it is, for I only just come on him lying like that, and when I called to him he didn't speak. Oh, sir, please come."

"Yes, yes, I'll come. Of course I'll come."

The kind-hearted old fellow hastened to the injured boy's side, and bent over him. Certainly the face was terribly white and drawn, though no marks were there to point to the manner in which the sufferer had come by his injury.

Just at this moment the injured urchin did a curious thing. His limbs became contorted as if by a sudden convulsion. At the same time he stretched out his arms from under the covering coat and clutched hysterically at the lower part of the lawyer's waistcoat.

Kindly but firmly the good man pressed the trembling limbs back into their former recumbent position ere he hurried off for medical assistance.

As soon as he was gone on his errand of mercy the unconscious boy got up, looked round about him cautiously to make sure no one was watching, then took to his heels and ran off in an opposite direction, closely followed by the brother with the black eye.

Not till they were safely back in Angel Court did the two stop. Then the black-eyed brother, otherwise Shanks, turned to his comrade in crime.

"How's that for a soft job, Peace? You got it all right, didn't yer?"

"Not 'arf!" And putting one finger to the side of his nose in approved fashion, Charles Peace pulled out of his pocket a massive gold chronometer and chain, the result of the convulsive clutch that had sent the kindly lawyer off in such a hurry to summon help.

Thus in a bound we get our first insight into the criminal side of Peace's character. Now let us look at another, and, in its way, equally important side of the queer personality which is the central figure of this life history.

From childhood his passion for music was wonderful. It never deserted him wholly, even in the last years of his existence.

His great instrument about this time was the violin. Among the few things his father took the trouble to teach him was the method of playing on this instrument.

But that was not enough for Peace. Carried away by the dramatic idea of doing something startling he soon evolved for himself a way of playing the fiddle all his own. Very shortly, when he was but fourteen years of age, he got the chance of airing his newly acquired gift in public.

Let us follow him on this his first public bid for recognition.

A dull, dismal December night in Sheffield. The pavements turned into mere puddles by the rain that falls ever in the same monotonous downpour. For the best part of the preceding day the gutters have been rushing torrents at either side of the sheet of slush that passed as roadway.

THE LIFE STORY OF CHARLES PEACE

Such is the night we may well picture to ourselves on which groups of drenched and draggled humanity pausing at the door of a small public-house had their attention arrested by a torn playbill stuck in the window.

Those who stopped to read it found that it was to announce the first appearance in that town of the "Great Etheopian Musician, the Modern Paganini," who would that night perform at the variety entertainment to be held on the first floor.

Most of those who entered the public-house took themselves off to see the show. In these days there were no music-halls in our modern acceptance of the term. To them a variety entertainment usually meant the wheezing of a fiddle in a bar parlour, some clog dancing, and a few doubtful songs. No wonder the announcement of the "Etheopian Paganini" attracted them to the upper room.

When the audience had taken their seats the landlord of the inn swaggered forward leading by the hand a curious creature, at which some of the more susceptible among the spectators shuddered.

It was a lad, to judge by the height and slimness of build, but the face was coal black except for the great irregular red slit, that marked the lips of a huge misshapen mouth. In his hand the lad held a curious instrument looking like a long stick down which was stretched a single piece of catgut supported on a wooden bridge after the manner of an ordinary violin.

No one in the audience had ever seen anything like it or the performer before. Instinctively after the first shock of surprise had worn off the audience settled themselves in for a real "good time."

"Ladies and Gentlemen," said the landlord, "this is the modern Etheopian Paganini, who will play a number of solos on his violin with one string. If any gentleman present doubts his ability to do so he is at liberty to examine the violin."

But no one took up the challenge. They were all too astounded at the strange appearance of the performer and far too impatient to hear what sort of sound he would product from so unlikely an instrument.

And then he commenced. The tunes were the old favorites, which only served to make the whole thing seem the more extraordinary.

For the first he played them holding the stick between his legs after the manner of a violoncello. Next, quick as lightning and right in the middle of a difficult passage, he had changed the position of the instrument. Now it was behind his back, and still the tune proceeded as though the feat were not really a marvelous one.

After that the violin was played in turn behind the performer's head, under his uplifted leg, at arm's length.

Then at last it was over. The applause burst in a deafening

roar that drowned and more than drowned the patter of rain drops on the glass of the crazy window.

Charles Peace, the modern Etheopian Paganini, had scored his first public triumph.

At the present moment there are still extant old playbills in which the "Etheopian Paganini" figures as trick violinist. Moreover, it is known that about this time Charles Peace even went so far in his bid for fame in the role of musician as to get together a sort of touring variety show, which only disbanded through lack of box office receipts. Had the venture proved successful, in all probability the youthful Charles Peace would have turned into an impressario instead of a criminal. As it was, the grim tutor poverty soon set to work to remind him all too forcibly how easy was money to make by other and less honest means.

For all that, be it said to Peace's credit, this interval in his life does seem to show a real attempt on his part to live rightly. Even poverty and its attendant temptations might have been successfully surmounted had it not been for two great set-backs, which turned the scale on the side of wrong. The first of these emanated from the very former playfellows who but a short while since had acknowledged him as leader.

Peace's rise in life—as it appeared to those who had known him formerly—excited no little envy on the part of his one time companions.

The street boys were not slow to take what advantage they could of the change in his fortunes. What was more, Peace was still no more than a lad, and with all an intelligent lad's sensitiveness to ridicule.

He was walking along Hollis Croft one day when he was set upon by a gang of his old cronies. Laughing and jeering at his odd appearance, they visited him with all the various forms of coarse torture they knew by experience to be most calculated to wound him.

"There goes the bogey man."

"What's the matter with your mouth?"

"Old Pag!"

One can almost hear these and such-like taunts echoing after him as he increases his pace more and more in a vain endeavor to outdistance his tormentors.

It seems to have been the last sneering reference to his performance on the violin, of which like many another greater artiste both before and since his time he may be supposed to have been somewhat vain, that at last drove him to desperation.

Smarting with the anger born of wounded pride, Peace turned on the one who last spoke and dealt him a violent blow on the face.

Reeling back, the other put his hand in his pocket. A moment later there was a flash and a report. Young Peace had been shot in his left hand.

At the hospital, whither he was hastily conveyed, three fingers had to be amputated.

And yet there are those who would dub him an abandoned, unscrupulous ruffian because in his after life he went about carrying loaded firearms. Nevertheless a period of several years elapsed between his maiming and the time when he finally took to crime as a means of livelihood.

How he occupied himself during this time is only roughly known.

His father died in 1845, and between then and 1851, when the first conviction is recorded against him, we know that at one part of the time he went to work in a button factory. At another he was errand boy at a carver, gilder, and picture framer's shop.

He still spent his off evenings earning odd money by his performances on the one-stringed fiddle at local penny gaffs and free-and-easys. It is certain that his first acquaintance with the art of theatrical make-up which he afterwards used to such good—or bad—effect in his criminal calling was made when watching the artistes "make up" for their turns at such public-house entertainments.

So matters went on year after year, the boy or lad being ever perched on the brink of criminality, ever learning the sordid lesson that forces itself on all in a like situation with an insistency that only the strong can bear up against—that there is greater present gain in knavery than in honest work.

Perhaps Charles Peace would have held his own against such specious promptings were it not for a second bit of ill-luck which seems finally to have worsted him in his struggle for a straightforward life.

In 1850, when he was eighteen years old and employed at the Mullsands Rolling Mill near Sheffield, he suffered a serious injury to his leg.

Up to then, since the death of his father, Peace had been making a real try to earn an honest living, and this notwithstanding his injured hand. He realised he must go to work for the sake of home and home ties. Hard the work might be, uncongenial in the highest degree. Still, it had to be done, for he was fatherless from the age of twelve.

Peace, the greatest ruffian of the nineteenth century, set to and did it. At least, he had a good try.

But fate, mocking his efforts, sent upon him the other bodily hurt that was finally to set the seal on his future way of life.

Some people said that the accident was caused by the fall of a piece of metal.

But Peace's own version of the story is that a fellow workman ran a piece of hot wire into him.

Whatever the real nature of the misfortune, it seems to have dealt the final and crushing blow to his determination of getting his living honestly.

Years afterwards, in discussing the incident, he would say, "Ah, I never cared to work after that."

Poor fellow, he has already been maimed, now he is lamed as well. Can we not find some sorrow for his case even while we condemn him?

At any rate the foregoing statement of his seems to coincide most significantly with the fact that the date of his first conviction was 1851, precisely one year after his accident.

With this date, then, we lose sight of Peace the child, Peace the musician. Henceforth his life history becomes that of Peace the burglar and murderer, the Master Criminal of the nineteenth century.

CHAPTER II.

Early Crimes

Peace's first detected theft may be looked upon as merely of the nature of an experiment to see if his hand had lost its cunning.

It was a theft of ladies' purses, followed closely by the "snatching" of a gentleman's watch at a Sheffield fair.

Charles was now something over eighteen years of age.

For the latter of the two above-mentioned offenses he was convicted, yet very soon was busy again. When he was nineteen— that is to say, within a few months of his first offense—he paid a midnight visit to the house of the mother of the future mayor of the town. He was evidently on the way to being an expert housebreaker, for he got into the place by climbing the portico, a method of attack that was always a favourite one of his. The robbery was not traced to him until some time afterwards, when, in trying to dispose of a brace of pistols, part of the missing property, he was caught, and paid for his lack of experience with a month's imprisonment.

Not such a bright start after all, one may say. But how many people do make bright starts in exceptionally difficult and tricky trades?

That he profited by the experience gained from these early failures we shall very soon see. One thing he learnt from them was to work as much as possible on his own. As a man and a full-blown criminal, apart from the small family circle which we shall hear of later, Peace had no real friend. The guiding principle of his life was to work alone. It has been said that he never even had an accomplice, but this must be untrue, otherwise how did he dispose of the proceeds of his numerous burglaries?

Moreover, he owed one at least of his convictions to the faithlessness of a "pal."

That he remained at large as long as he did after being wanted for murder is undoubtedly due to his strict adherence to the principle of keeping himself to himself. Were it not for the "pals" who "split" Scotland Yard might close its doors.

In his after life most of Peace's business was done between eight o'clock in the evening and midnight. Twelve o'clock usually found him in bed, a useful rule when he was living a fleeting existence at coffee taverns and doss-houses. His host could always swear that his lodger was between the sheets if the police suggested that he must have come in at an unearthly hour—which is only another way of saying that Peace generally relied for his security on the stupidity of others.

When he came out after his "month," he seems to have realised that if he wished the police to turn their eyes from him he must at any rate pretend to resume an honest trade if only as a blind.

Accordingly he launched out into a small carver and gilder's shop, as well as continuing his musical performances of an evening, though the very fact that he found the money to start himself in business at so early an age suggests that his activities even then were far greater than the police ever suspected.

Later on in his career more than one unfortunate householder had good reason to know that Charles Peace had to be caught before he could be convicted.

Besides, when Peace first set out on the Rogue's March the police were far from being an efficient organisation.

Criminal investigation was in its infancy. Except when he stupidly blundered the music-hall artiste was more than a match for the trained watchman.

Released from prison, he went back to crime just as a workman goes to his daily task, only in his case he had become both more astute and more ambitious in the interval.

The first few robberies that he perpetrated on gaining his freedom were in themselves small affairs. But they served a very important purpose.

They engendered in their perpetrator as ever-growing ambition.

Soon Peace got dreams of enlarging his scope of operations. Perhaps Sheffield was becoming unpleasantly familiar with his ugly face.

At last he left his native town to go into "business" on a larger scale.

He moved to Bradford. It is to this town that we must look for the record of his first really daring burglary. Let us admit at once the facts concerning it are as disgraceful as any in the man's history.

For the incident about to be recorded, as of many others in his career, it is difficult or impossible to find any excuse whatever.

Peace had been in Bradford but a very short time when he spotted the house of a well-known Bradford woollen merchant as a likely one for his depredations.

The house was of the kind that would be owned by a commercial aristocrat of Yorkshire. It was staffed by something like a dozen servants, and was, in fact, just the "crib" which appeals to the average "cracksman."

Peace did not bungle over effecting self-introductions in his new town. Knowing that he was about to break fresh ground he was careful to present that appearance of honesty and propserity so successful to the success of his plots

Sheffield had not been an unprofitable speculation from a financial point of view. He had fifty or sixty pounds at his command, to say nothing of a wardrobe designed both to attract and to deceive.

He gave himself out as the musical offspring of well-to-do parents. He lived, he said, by his violin. He gave music lessons—this was his story—and anything he lacked by reason of an unfortunate scarcity of pupils he made up by taking concert engagements.

His time was thus fully accounted for. When "Mr. John Ward"—his present alias—was not to be seen in the daytime inquisitive neighbors were easily assured. He was attending upon his many pupils.

If, on the other hand, the lady next door wondered why it was that Mr. Ward came home so late at night—well, the audience insisted on many encores, and thus the concert was not over till the small hours of the morning.

As a matter of fact, most of his absences from home were spent in carefully mapping and planning out the whole or greater part of the city and its surrounding suburbs. He took daily walks for the express purpose of noting down the most likely "cribs," and as it happened the woollen merchant's house was among the earliest and most likely ones to be spotted.

But how was the crib to be cracked? It seemed to be defended at all points.

At length, after many a long and earnest deliberation worthy of a better cause, Peace came to the conclusion that it was only the old, old key that would unlock the mansion door. The allegiance of one of the indoor servants must be enlisted.

So he made it his business to hang about the roads and lanes near by till, finally, by sheer impudence, he managed to make the acquaintance of a servant named Fanny Blinkhorn.

Bit by bit Peace managed to first ingratiate himself, later to firmly establish himself in the woman's confidence. Presently it came to "walking out" together and it is to be feared the misguided Fanny

THE LIFE STORY OF CHARLES PEACE

did what many another fickle young lady had done and lived to regret; she sent the hum-drum mechanic who had been her former lover about his business, preferring the superior though totally untried attractions of the "musician."

Then Peace was duly introduced to the servants' hall, to the great astonishment of its occupants, an astonishment which he hastened to turn into warm approbation by gallant behaviour.

Soon he had become a welcome visitor all round. His ugly face, so far from sounding the danger signal to the unwary occupants of the servants' hall, was to them an inexhaustible source of amusement.

He could twist it into contortions that made the watchers ache with laughter. As a singer of comic songs he was grand company.

A few days more and he and the hapless Fanny were engaged, and the girl had parted with her small savings.

All the time the rascal was straining his ears for information.

Soon he discovered among other things that several hundred pounds' worth of silver was locked into a chest every night and deposited in the butler's pantry. Doors and windows were fitted with burglar alarms, and a loaded gun was kept handy for intruders. Outside a big Newfoundland dog kept guard on the house day and night.

All these details Peace noted down, and laid his plans accordingly. A favourable opportunity soon presented itself. It was the time of the New Year festivities. He learned from Fanny Blinkhorn that on a certain night all the family except two children and a governess would be away from home. Curious, wasn't it? The date coincided with his birthday.

He suggested a supper and a dance in the servant's hall, and, the arrangement approved of, the rascal considerately brought his violin.

All sorts of delicacies were provided, and "Mr. John Ward" was to contribute a present of wine.

What excellent company Mr. Ward was, to be sure! Loud and long were the revels. Merry dances charmed away the hours. Whilst the company danced "Mr. Ward" fiddled for all he was worth—and watched his prey like a weasel. His wicked little eyes were gleaming like coals. What a funny little man he was.

After the dance, supper. More wine was uncorked, and many a joke was cracked as everybody drank full bumpers to everybody else, "Mr. Ward" included. And then—what more natural—the company dropped off to sleep one by one. The only sober man was he who had been the life and soul of the party. No one seemed to wonder why "Mr. Ward" had contributed the wine.

The blithe fiddler quickly became the desperate thief. He slipped away to the butler's pantry and secured as much of the silver as he could conveniently carry. Then he cut the wires of the burglar alarm, secured the windows and the doors, wrenched the lid off the plate chest, poisoned the dog, concealed his booty—and went to sleep as calmly as the others.

When the morning dawned what a commotion—what confusion and alarm! The servants are frightened out of their wits. The butler is beside himself with horror and anxiety. A burglary has been committed during the night. The silver has gone!

Off goes the butler to break the news to his master and mistress. "Mr. Ward" is terribly put about. He soothes the women and takes wise counsel with the men. Finally, having kindly offered to warn the police, he takes his leave and his plunder and departs!

The theft was not brought home to the perpetrator till many years afterwards, when a woman named Blinkhorn sought admission to a London workhouse and confessed that Peace had committed the crime.

She told a terrible story. After the crime Peace had been artful enough to still keep up his friendly connection with the mansion. He continued to visit the foolish girl who had been his dupe, a series of attentions that had continued even after she had left her situation and right down to a time when she was robbed of her attractiveness.

The silver was never recovered.

CHAPTER III.

First Term of Penal Servitude

After the Bradford robbery, which was committed about the year 1854, Peace lay low for a time.

Doubtless he favoured another town with his presence, but when he had made quite sure the danger had blown over he returned. This time he re-took his old Sheffield blind of carrying on the trade of a carver and gilder.

The occupation served as well as another to cover the true nature of his nocturnal depredations. His appearance, too, had undergone a change, as we shall see.

One of the first things he proceeded to do was to take steps to protect himself against suspicious pawnbrokers by a simple plan, which in his case proved none the less effective.

He took two women into his employ to help him to get rid of the "swag." One of them was the same Fanny Blinkhorn who had already helped him on the occasion previously narrated.

They were installed in a small house from which the "agency" was conducted. Soon business grew and expanded.

As a carver and gilder Peace found it convenient to simulate falling on bad times. Thus the neighbors were not surprised at the gentleman next door being continually away from home on the look out for odd wrk.

Let us follow him on one of these tramps.

Those standing at the street corner would see a queer undersized figure come lurching out of the doorway of the little shop.

A second glance would show the man to be of reality younger than he looked at first sight, but that was soon accounted for by the

THE LIFE STORY OF CHARLES PEACE

dress proclaiming him a seaman. The hardships of life had worn him down.

Away he would walk with the rolling gate of the sea, and if the watchers were sharp-eyed they may have noticed he had had the misfortune to lose an arm. In place of it was a wooden substitute fitted with an iron hook at the end.

We who have had the advantage of his acquaintance from birth have no difficulty in recognizing the one-armed sailor. But the good citizens of Bradford were not so fortunate, and in due time they were made to realise the fact by the painful if monotonous process of loss of property.

Let us wait and see the man's tactics when darkness has fallen. The following typical instance of one of his burglaries will suffice to reveal the man better than many words.

The house he had spotted was a large semi-detached one lying a little way back from the road in its own small strip of garden.

The one-armed sailor crept stealthily round the street corner, gave one long and searching glance to make sure no one was in sight, then suddenly rising his wooden arm made a leap and a cast with the hook at the end of it at the low hanging branch of an elm tree that overhung the back garden wall.

There was a jerk, the sound of snapping twigs, and the hook had taken firm hold. Swarming up into the tree lithe as a cat the burglar waited a minute to make sure his movements had not been noticed, then slipped down noiselessly on to the gravel path of the back garden, across it, and the intervening vegetable patch, and had gained the kitchen window.

The false arm was hastily cast aside. It was in reality only a hollow contrivance concealing beneath it a perfectly sound limb.

Taking from his pocket a keen-bladed knife Peace skilfully slipped back the catch of the window and entered.

Another obstacle to be surmounted, this time the kitchen door. It was locked on the outside. This time Peace brought to light a picklock. There was a rasp, a click, the obstacle was no more.

A glance in the front room. Nothing of the nature of a safe or bureau that might contain the money there. Very well. It must be on the first floor.

He glided up the staircase.

At last the first floor was reached. Ah! There was the writing-desk sure enough. He darted forward and tried the lid. Locked!

Good! He had found the hiding-place of the hoard. It was well. A fierce grin of anticipation o'erspread his face.

The flash of a small jemmy. Crack! The lid of the desk went with a snap. Another instant and his fingers were on the golden store within. Feverishly he was cramming the money into his pockets when the shrill scream of a police whistle rent the air while the screwed up door resounded with thud upon thud.

With a snarl of fury Peace sprang up and ran to the open window.

Too late. Already he could see dark forms flitting to and fro on the pale moonlit strip of grass without.

Trapped, then, was he?

Bringing to light a fully-loaded revolver, Peace cocked the trigger and took deliberate aim through the open window. The shot was never fired. At the very moment Peace tightened his finger on the trigger of the revolver, the dark form of the man in the garden below moved off in response to a hurried call from the back of the house.

Not one second did the burglar wait. Quick as a flash he was out through the window and clinging by the finger-tips to the ledge, his body swaying periously over the path beneath. Then he dropped.

Ah, he is down all of a heap! He has injured hiself badly, mortally perhaps. At all events his capture is inevitable.

But no, he has struggled to his feet again and is off with the bound of a tiger-cat.

After that police whistles blew in vain. In vain blue-coated constables and sergeants scoured every square inch of the house and grounds for sign or clue of the daring midnight intruder.

It was one more score for the future Bannercross murderer, one more step successfully traversed on the road that was to lead him in due time to the foot of the gallows, and thence up the rickety ladder that led to the drop and the end of earthly existence.

And Peace in the quietude of his bedroom over the mean little carver's and gilder's shop might sit and count his spoils and gloat to his heart's content.

A poor, one-armed sailor in search of a job! Truly a marvel in criminality. He had even sought out and regained possession of the false arm before leaving the scene of his night's exploit. There lay the dummy on the chair by the bedside half covered with crumpled bank notes. Could but the police have seen it.

In face of such a record as this it will hardly come as a piece of surprising intelligence that during the two years Peace remained in Bradford he extracted from it the foundations of a small fortune.

Night after night he carried out similarly successful raids. Some of the stolen property he disposed of at a small general shop, but his two women agents working under his able supervision got rid of all the more valuable articles for him.

He "worked" mostly at private houses, helping himself to jewellery, plate, or anything else that was portable and worth carrying away.

Sometimes, as we have seen, he made a haul of bank notes. These he cashed by the simple, and at the time safe, because little known, expedient of buying bottles of spirits at neighboring towns, and using them in payment.

Where the number of notes to be disposed of made the task of getting rid of them dangerous, he would send one of his "agents" with them to a "bank-note specialist," or species of "fence" (receiver of stolen goods), who earned a fat, if somewhat precarious, living by judiciously altering the numbers on them at a heavy commission.

Once the numbers of the notes were altered they could not be traced to their source, and thus the holder of them was rendered practically safe.

The transaction usually cost Peace a sovereign a note. But what did it matter? Money was cheap. No matter how bad the times were, the carver and gilder was never known to want.

Yet still Peace was barely twenty years old, though he was already one of the most dangerous criminals of his day. He never went abroad without his loaded revolver, though he used to insist, even to the very end, and probably with truth, that he had never wilfully injured those who were unfortunate enough to interfere with his expeditions.

Two Bradford policemen had the misfortune to encounter him on those unequal terms. He inflicted no wounds. He simply fired wide at his would-be captors and made off in the confusion.

For all that, Bradford soon became too hot for him. On the second occasion on which he brought the pistol into play a reward of fifty pounds was offered for the capture of "Charles Frederick Peace," and accordingly he fled.

From Bradford Peace retreated on Sheffield, the scene of his early lapses from virtue and his first exploits in crime. The year was 1854. It was in the house of his mother that he sought refuge.

He was soon at work again. As before, he devoted himself to the contents of gentlemen's houses. Sheffield contributed most of the plunder, but he occasionally went long distances in order to make raids on houses he had spotted during the walks it was ever his custom to take.

All the time he kept in touch with his Bradford confederates, who still saw to the disposal of the contents of the heavy parcels of booty that came at regular intervals.

Probably few honest business firms have started a more sound investment in the way of a branch business than this one of Charles Peace. The upkeep was small, for he was never over generous; the trade done in stolen goods was immense, and last, but not least, he knew that in Bradford he had always got a safe hiding-place from the police should the worst come to the worst.

Little wonder if, in face of so seemingly perfect organization, he felt comparatively safe. Yet in reality it was just about now that his first long term of penal servitude was looming ahead of him.

It came upon him suddenly, as might be supposed, in this way. The year was 1854, the scene of the arrest a little first floor room of a tumble-down house situate in one of the lowest side alleys of Sheffield.

The house was the official residence of a fence with whom Peace, breaking through his general rule, had decided to do business in person.

The man had pushed open the street door, and was slouching up the flight of rotten wooden stairs. So old and badly built were they that even he, with all his cat-like agility, could not prevent them from creaking under his weight as he ascended.

Perhaps the creaking of the stairs was one of the accepted institutions of the establishment, acting as it did in lieu of bell or knocker at the front door. However that may be, as the sounds of creaking commenced, a door at the top of the staircase was opened about half-an-inch, while a croaking voice from the other side demanded:

"Who's there?"

"It's I," said Peace. "No fear. It ain't the rozzers this time. Got something here to do a deal with you over."

Burglar and receiver stood facing each other in the grimy room from which the dust and dirt that stuck to the windows shut out all but the merest glint of daylight.

Peace put down the parcel on the rough deal table and undid the paper. At the flash of the silver that was revealed within the fence could not restrain a gasp of avarice.

Here was a man worth doing business with indeed. Let but the world produce a few more crooks of this sort, and even a poor downtrodden receiver of stolen goods might live.

But hark! Even before the two could fall to discussing the terms of their bargain the words had died on their lips.

They were silent now, silent as the grave, scarcely daring to breathe, while their ears were strained to breaking point.

Was it fancy? Surely it must have been, for all was silent now.

"Lock the door," whispered Peace, only to break off again as the dread sound occurred for the second time.

The stairs were creaking!

And then the blow fell. With a click the door of the room was thrown open, and four uniformed constables dashed in. It was all so sudden and unexpected that even the resourceful Peace was thrown off his guard, and had not time to whip out his revolver ere he was overwhelmed and pinioned hand and foot.

In vain he tried to fight himself free of his captors. For once he was fairly outnumbered and outmatched, the direct result of breaking through his golden rule to leave all such dangerous work as the present to confederates on whom less suspicion would be likely to fall.

But to moralise on that now was of little avail even if he felt in the mood for it. While he was being captured the fence had shared a like fate.

Down to the street the two of them were led or pushed. By the pavement a cab was waiting for them. What could have been more thoughtful on the part of the police?

THE LIFE STORY OF CHARLES PEACE

A quick drive in it, then the police station, the charge, the cells. Next morning the magisterial inquiry, followed by committal to the assizes.

That time it was no mere month's hard Peace was in for. In due course he found himself a convict sentenced to five years' penal servitude, a sentence by no means over-long even according to present-day notions, as we must admit if we consider the circumstances.

All the same, the length of it indicates this: that the police had made what they would consider quite an important capture—as indeed they had.

CHAPTER IV.
Peace the Convict.

Of Peace's life in prison either whil undrgoing this or subsequent sentences there are only fitful glimpses vouchsafed to his friends in after years when he was in communicative mood.

In these days a comparatively beneficial law in inflicting on him the first of these long sentences would have recognized in the convict a man of the very type for whom the Borstal system has been devised. True, he would have been in prison just the same. But he would have undergone such a process of scientific remodelling that at the end of his term he would probably have been sent back to society a more or less valuable member. Such, at any rate, is the aim and intention of the Borstal system. And good intentions are in themselves hopeful signs even in prison management.

In Peace's days things were different. There was no idea of reform. The law took no thought of the man. Punishment was the only consideration. It makes one wonder what Peace might have been after four years of sound training. His many talents formed an excellent groundwork, but they were all thrown away.

Previous to his sentence and while still he was kicking his heels in the city goal awaiting trial, what he took to be a chance of escape presented itself.

Always alert, always prepared to jump at the slightest vestige of an opportunity for freedom, his quick eyes spied a rope's end dangling down from the top of the prison wall one day when he was at exercise.

He made a sudden dash. There was a hoarse shout of rage and chagrin from the warder in charge, and he rushed forward just as Peace, trusting all to the firmness of the rope's fastening, seized it and swarmed up it like a monkey.

Up, up he went; then, just as the top of the wall appeared to be within reach of his outstretched arm, there was a sickening bump. The rope had got loose on the other side, only to catch on to something and hitch itself tight again the next minute. Peace had never let it go. Even yet he might manage to clamber up it a second time and elude the authorities.

Once more he was swarming up, just as the warder, reaching spot. made a furious leap and got hold of his foot.

Peace was caught! But, no! The boot had come off in the officer's hand. The prisoner would escape yet.

Another frantic haul on the rope from Peace, a fierce drawing up of the legs out of reach of his captor. He was well up the wall again. He was free! A second time the rope gave under him. With a savage wrench the prisoner was seized as he fell backwards.

His attempt had been thwarted, but only just.

It was Peace's first effort in the direction of prison breaking, and, like that other and greater one that he was destined to make later on in his career, it had failed.

Behold, then, the youthful gallows bird in penal servitude at the early age of twenty-two. A mature age this for such dangerous propensities as he was already exhibiting At first he worked in the garden at Wakefield Prison. Monotonous days those of weeding and digging. They gave him time to think, and thinking was bad for Charles Peace.

By-and-by, he was sent to work in the prison as a mat-maker. All day long he sat "teeming" the rough fibre. At night he lay in his cell, his restless brain longing for something to do.

It was there that he taught himself the elements of the carver's art. There was nothing else to do, so he set about making paper models. By degrees he became more and more proficient, till he could play such wonderful tricks with bits of paper that the prison officials recognised in him something of the born architect. When he was not modelling he was scratching designs on the wall of his cell. Wasted talents indeed!

But the life was wearing the man to distraction. He began to devise plans for escape, and at last hit upon one as daring as anything of its kind.

One evening he watched his opportunity and slipped out of the building in which his cell was situated. He was a small, undersized youth, but as active as an eel. He found an open door and crept away.

Outside in the yard he was confronted with a low wall. He scrambled up, ran along the top, and got on to the roof of a house occupied by the prison doctor, whose name was Milner. For the moment he was baffled. Freedom was no nearer.

But Peace's fertile wits never failed him. He quickly tore a few slates off the roof, and dropped into the garret. He was safe for the moment. What he wanted now was a suit of clothes.

Down he went to a bedroom. Whilst he was rummaging about he was startled by a tremendous hullaballoo outside. which announced to all whom it concerned that a prisoner had escaped.

Quick as thought he climbed to the top of a wardrobe where he lay at full length beneath the ceiling.

THE LIFE STORY OF CHARLES PEACE

High and low the warders searched. At last they found him, and he was taken back to his cell.

Needless to say, the present was by no means the criminal's only taste of convict life.

Part of one of Peace's sentences was served at Dartmoor, where he left behind him an excellent memento—a carved pulpit.

Poor Peace, unappreciated outside prison, seems to have been highly valued within. At Wakefield his turn for wood-carving was encouraged, and, as a Government investment, it proved exceedingly valuable when he reached Dartmoor. At another period of his penal experiences he carved a font for Wandsworth prison.

For all that, there were influences bred in the man's bones which every now and then hurled him down to the depths of degradation.

He once led a mutiny at Portland Prison which earned him a dose of the "cat."

The convicts had been escorted back from their work at the great stone quarries connected with the settlement, and were about to be searched by the warder told off for that purpose, when, at a signal from Peace, they made a concerted dash for those who held guard over them.

Foremost amongst the mutineers was their ringleader, and soon, to the consternation of the warders, it became evident that the attack had been organised by a master hand.

Every convict had managed to secrete under his uniform a small but sharp clip of stone picked up at the quarries. Gripping these after the manner of improvised knives, they made so fierce an onslaught that, but for the arrival of reinforcements of the armed guard in the nick of time, it is hard to say what might not have occurred.

As it was, when Peace's punishment, in the form of a good stiff dose of the "cat," had been duly administered, it was thought wise to remove him from his fellows, over whom he seemed to have acquired so strong and so disquieting an influence.

It so happened that about this time the convicts were being sent from England to help in the making of fortifications on the rock of Gibralter. Peace was sent thither with a batch of refractory criminals. It was his solitary excursion beyond the British Isles.

While working at Gibralter he was reported by a warder named Baynes for some offence. Thereafter Baynes was a marked man. Not a doubt of it. Peace was ever a nasty customer to get on the wrong side of. Henceforth his mind was concentrated on the evolution of some means by which he could wreak vengeance on his custodian.

It is said that in this plot Peace took into his confidence a certain fellow convict named Sims. Sims like himself had a "down" on the warder. Naturally the master criminal thought himself safe enough in enlisting his services.

The plot the two concocted between them was old enough and mean enough in all conscience. Nevertheless, it is one which prisoners have often worked off on unsuspecting warders—the luring of others into indiscreet kindness in order to make capital out of their subsequent undoing.

The scheme was that Sims, who had been getting on distinctly better with Baynes of late, should, by a process of "soft soaping," lure the official into some piece of personal generosity which would amount to a breach of prison regulations. This done, he was to communicate the fact to Peace, who would lose no time in bearing the tale to the governor of the convict settlement.

Peace knew at the start it would be no use for himself to try and draw out the hated official in any such way. Their mutual ill-will was far too well marked for that. Hence the convict's agreement to receiving help from a fellow "lag."

The way Sims went to work was simple. He feigned a sudden loss of appetite combined with apathy. There were frequent occasions on which he seemed to break down and show all the signs of a mind on the point of succumbing to his terrible lot.

At first the warder (who was not at heart a bad man) tried to get the convict to see the doctor. No; he would not go. He did not feel he could stand being in hospital, he declared. His mind was on the verge of giving way as it was. Add this and it would snap.

Baynes began to take rather a morbid interest in the case. After all, when a man is down, be he free or fettered, he has still sufficient of the human element in him to arouse our sympathies—if we have any at all to be aroused.

Unfortunately for himself our warder had. Presently he was cajoled into lending a willing ear to the wailing of Sims. He wanted a meal, not the horrible prison soup and skilly or the nauseating bitter cocoa which was all with a little fat bacon that the prison allowed to the workers in stone quarries. He wanted a snack of something to eat which would remind him of the outside world. He didn't mind what. If it was only a slice of cake it would do—and he might perhaps know of a place where quite a large quantity of tobacco was stored, very good tobacco, too.

The scheme worked. Sims' goaler arrived one day with something wrapped up in a handkerchief which was surreptitiously passed into the convict's cell, half of it to be eaten with great gusto, the rest to be kept as evidence when Peace saw fit to "split" on the unhappy official.

And Peace was not long about it. That same morning as soon as ever the two caught sight of one another on the way to chapel the signal was passed between them which had been arranged beforehand so as to let Peace know that all was ready for the warder's undoing.

First thing after chapel Peace saw the governor and split. It was as mean an act as it was detestable, and one can only understand it on the part of one of Charles Peace's crooked code of morality.

The governor heard the allegation with a stern frown on his

hard face. A warder guilty of smuggling food into the prison! That was Peace's story, but how could he corroborate it? Sims? Very good. Sims should be sent for immediately.

And now Peace's fellow convict has arrived on the scene.

The governor is addressing him sternly.

"Is it true that you have received surreptitious presents of food from the warder in charge of your cell? Is it true that you have come to any arrangement with him of such a sort? Is there a word of truth in this story of your fellow convict?"

"No! No! No!" As the answers come out one after another Peace opens his eyes to stare at his "confederate" in sheer amazement, an amazement which turns swiftly enough to a glare of deadly enmity as he realises the truth. It is he himself, not the warder, who is being let down. Sims has indeed come to an arrangement with his goaler, but it is not to obtain the latter his dismissal but to bring down upon Peace's head dire punishment.

Perhaps this man who is now contradicting his statements meant at first to stand by his fellow convict, and has only yielded to lavish promises made by the warder within the last half-hour. Perhaps he meant to let Peace down from the first. What matter? Whichever may be the case the future Bannercross murderer's mind is made up.

Sims shall pay for his treachery with his life.

Yet the day of retribution is not to be yet, nor for some little while. There lie in the interval many days of punishment for Peace.

And then—at last—the day does come.

CHAPTER V.

The Death of Sims

It comes when by some mischance the two convicts have been drafted into the same gang at the fortification works.

Peace recognizes Sims in a flash as he joins the gang, and inwardly notes the chance that has at last come his way. The other convict at sight of the former friend whom he has betrayed quails and takes a quick step backward——all to no avail. A stern rebuke from the warder in charge sends him trembling back to his place.

Peace is grinning fiendishly. He has seen it all, the frenzied terror, the half-savage command for Sims to fall back into line. Who can tell how he enjoyed the moments that followed? He was getting his own back at last. Only partially, so far, but wait. Before the evening he might have it altogether. Who could tell?

Still with the same dark gleam of evil in his eyes, he went about his task of hauling up the huge blocks of stone wherewith to build the immense wall on which the convicts were engaged.

And then the crucial moment! The opportunity had come.

Sims had been sent up to the top of the wall—that is to a height of nearly fifteen feet above the solid stone foundation on which the others were standing—to push a block of stone into place as it was let down from a pulley overhead.

With trembling steps the man ascended the narrow ladder till he stood on the top of the wall, on the summit of a ledge of stone not eighteen inches wide. He must have known what would happen, for all below saw, and many, had they dared, would have remarked how he shuddered as he bent to his task.

And then, with the characteristic agility we have come to know so well, Peace was up and after him.

In vain the warder dashed at him to prevent what was about to happen. Peace was up the fifteen-foot ladder almost at a bound and on the top of the wall face to face with Sims.

The frightened group of convicts beneath watched what followed in terrified silence.

For a moment the two enemies stood regarding one another. Then they closed for deadly combat. Somehow, while the danger of attack had only been hanging over Sims it had seemed to paralyse him with morbid fear. Now that the thing had become an accomplished reality the convict seemed to acquire new manhood and courage.

He braced himself to meet the onslaught of the master criminal and took firm stand on the narrow ledge as his assailant advanced.

Then the fight commenced in earnest. At first the two fought with fists, hitting parrying, jabbing, hacking. But the wall was too narrow for that to continue for long.

Instinctively the two realised that, if it were to continue, one or other of them would fall over through sheer accident. As the thought came home to them they rushed in anew on one another and closed in a desperate lock.

Peace was a Yorkshireman, and so knew most of the well-known falls common to north country wrestling, but here a surprise was in store for him. No sooner had he closed with his antagonist than he realised that as much, if not more, could be said for the other.

As a matter of fact, Sims was undergoing his term of incarceration for mortally injuring a fellow workman in a drunken wrestling brawl.

Little as they knew it they were two of a kind. As the terrible bout was played out on the top of the wall the little group of spectators beneath felt their horror in the scene melting away into sheer maddening interest.

Now Sims was trying desperately for the inside hitch. Would he get it? If so Peace would be over the wall in a matter of five seconds.

One and all the convicts beneath held their breath as they watched the limbs of the two perform move and counter-move.

Peace had foiled his antagonist in his attempt to obtain mastery, and was now himself making a desperate attempt to accomplish the other's destruction. Nearer and nearer the edge of the wall he had

ON THE TOP OF THE WALL PEACE AND HIS DEADLY ENEMY CLOSED FOR COMBAT.

Sims. More and more did the unhappy man's body sway on the verge of almost certain death when there came a sharp report.

In a trice all concerned realised what was the cause of it. The armed guard had been called to the rescue.

Mad with passion as he was Peace was forced to realise that to persist in his attempt would mean to him the certainty of being shot. With a growl of baffled rage he let go his hold of his victim just as the guard, rushing up to the foot of the wall, levelled their carbines full upon him.

Once again defeat. Once more punishment. Peace went through it like a stoic. But later, one night when the convicts were being called in from work unusually early on account of the sudden onset of a thick mist, one of them was found to be missing.

It was not Peace. For a wonder he was there with the rest. He had not attempted to break away. What was more he was smiling grimly—more grimly still when he heard the name of the missing man—Sims.

Sims was found next day—dead. He had pitched over a spur of rock whither it would seem he must have climbed in an attempt to escape under cover of the sea fog.

He had missed his footing and battered his brains out on the ground beneath, the very death Peace had intended should have been his many days before. Yet it would be unfair to lay the blame for the man's death at Peace's door. True, one never knows. Indeed one can only read of the master criminal's exploits to feel more and more as one goes on what a comparatively little part one can really know of all he did during his varied life.

Yet Sims' death may well have been an accident, albeit a rare coincidence to boot. Coincidences do happen, none the less, so that we ought not to go out of our way to assume Peace's responsibility for a murder of which he may well have been innocent.

In due time Peace regained his liberty. He and Baynes each went their separate ways. Probably neither gave a thought to the probability of their ever meeting again. Why should they? It was so unlikely?

Yet years afterwards the two were destined to come together once more, and under unusually dramatic circumstances. Peace was then the Bannercross fugitive.

One day he was hurrying across London Bridge when he saw a face he thought he knew. Without waiting for a second glance he fled.

The face was that of Warder Baynes.

But to return to the time of Peace's first long sentence. After serving four years of it he was discharged. The prison gates had hardly closed behind him when he was once more scouring the country for plunder.

This brings us to the period when he was twenty-six years of age. About this time, in 1858, he fell in with a widow named Hannah Ward. He met her while tramping the country carrying her infant son, who will figure in this life history later on under the name of Willie Ward or Peace. The woman was in a state of utter destitution resting by a canal bank.

More, it is to be feared, with a view to establishing another of his criminal agencies for the disposal of stolen property than with any better motive, he showed her kindness of sorts.

It is this Hannah Ward whom we find figuring with him in Hanley under the name of Hannah Peace.

From Hanley the two moved on to Worksop, and from thence after the perpetration of numerous and highly successful robberies they migrated to Sheffield. Once during this time Charles Peace called on his mother with a view to the three of them settling down under the maternal root tree, but the house was known and too closely watched to be safe.

So in the end another abode was chosen, from whence Peace proceeded to renew his acquaintance with Bradford and systematically to overhaul and re-cast his "branch business."

Once more the old tricks were pressed into the service. Once more he was the disguised artisan during the daytime and the burglar at night. Soon the authorities were again on his track.

All over the country the police began to hear of his numerous exploits and became more and more wary. A constable, seeing a little wizened man dart through the door of the private bar of a public-house with suspicious haste, remembered how his mates were one the look-out for a daring robber answering to the suspect's description. Accordingly he had the 'cuteness to put his head round the same door, just in time to watch his man sneak a quantity of cigars from a box on the counter, as also some loose money lying near by, and make his escape by the other entrance.

Soon the ambitious policeman was racing down the street in hot pursuit of the fugitive.

But the constable might have saved himself the trouble. We know Charlie quite well enough by now to be sure which way such a race as that would end.

It was not long ere our friend in blue was glad to sit down on a doorstep and mop his face with his ample pocket handkerchief. The hint was enough to send Peace off for a change of air in Hull, from whence in due time he made his way to York to astonish the worthy inhabitants of that historic city with a series of the most daring burglaries that had ever been known in the locality.

The proceeds of these robberies were sent to Hull, where they were quickly disposed of. Nothing was allowed to accumulate.

After some months in racking Yorkshire, Peace became Parker, and moved to Manchester. He was accompanied by Hannah Ward, who was soon installed in an eating-house that had been taken for her at a Bank Top.

For a time everything went well. The great warehouses, all of them stuffed to the roof with costly material, presented a splendid field for Peace's "talents." But one day something happened which brought in its trail serious disaster—from the burglar's point of view. He was going along the street, when he was recognised by an old "lag" who had met him in prison.

The incident would seem insignificant enough, but Peace knew better. Splitting on pals is quite a favourite wheeze of old lags, by which they seek to impress the authorities with the genuineness of their own reformation.

Moreover, Peace soon had good reason to know that the police were paying him unusual attention. Just about this time a young policeman found a parcel of stolen property in a drainpipe.

He at once took it to the police-station, where it was identified as part of the proceeds of a burglary. Without loss of time the parcel was replaced in the drain, and several officers were told off to await the arrival of the fox.

By-and-by they saw approaching a peculiar little man with a big head and a strikingly ugly face. The drain was in the middle of a piece of waste ground, and the little man calmly sat down a few yards away—presumably to admire the scenery.

Presently he crept closer to the drain—and closer—and closer still. Clearly it was not altogether scenery that attracted him. In the meantime the police in hiding close by had recognized their man.

Just as he was in the act of taking the parcel from the drain they pounced on the little gentleman with the ugly face, and hauled him off to the police-station.

Peace fought like a tiger for freedom. Then a curious thing happened. A gentleman who was passing along interpreted the scuffle into a violent assault on a helpless prisoner. He even followed the party to the police-station, where he launched out into an indignant protest against such proceedings.

The inspector took it very calmly. Suddenly he looked up from his papers, and, with a twinkle in his eye, said: "Do you happen to know who the prisoner is?"

The kind gentleman did not know. In any case——

"Then I'll tell you," said the inspector. "He's a notorious burglar named Charles Peace."

But Peace gave his name as "George Park" under which alias he was again tried and sent to penal servitude, this time for seven years.

With Peace's liberation at Sheffield begins the second and by far the most dramatic part of his career. Indeed in the life history of no other criminal can so many stirring incidents be found crowded

THE LIFE STORY OF CHARLES PEACE

over a short space of time than are to be found in the last three years of Peace's existence. It is upon the description of the most thrilling of these that we now enter.

CHAPTER VII.
The Shadow of the Gallows

Upon the daring burglar's liberation he did a thing few less forceful men would have cared to have done. He opened a picture-framing establishment in the High Street, with Hannah Ward as his partner.

It is here for the first time that we come across his queer liking for animals, a liking which at the time receives its assurance of genuineness and finds a ready counterpart both in the history of Wainwright, the English poet and poisoner, and of Lacenaire, the noted French criminal, whose love of cats was prodigious.

Peace's backyard was quite a menagerie of parrots and other feathered creatures, to say nothing of several yelping curs and a family of rabbits.

Later in life he was destined to be the owner of a pony, to which he became desperately attached. Of this more in its proper place.

For the present let us confine ourselves to his new business venture.

The shop did not pay. It would not be very difficult to find many reasons why such a venture should not succeed. The most probable explanation is that the police took so much interest in the welfare of the ex-convict that he became over-anxious.

In the possible event of his return to business being a genuine attempt at reform on Peace's part, he would have to be regarded in the light of one more victim to the not altogether satisfactory system of police surveillance of old criminals still in vogue at the present time.

For some little while our man was—or pretended to be—really in earnest in his attempts to lead a new life. He became a regular attendant at chapel. He even attracted the attention of several benevolent people who were so struck with his protestations of ardent reform that they regarded him as a prodigy of regeneration.

Rightly or wrongly, the police thought otherwise. They favoured the penitent carver with so much of their company, and incidentally saw to it that his previous history became so well known to those with whom he did business, that at last Peace decided there was nothing for it but to leave the city, and the shop in High Street was given up.

As one reason for hoping that this new phase of Peace's was a genuine attempt to become honest, it may be noted that about this time no startling burglaries took place in the locality.

After closing the shop at Sheffield, Peace decided to go to Darnall, a village a few miles outside the town.

All unknown to himself the book of fate was sealed and closed on the day he decided to make that change. It heralded in a new and terrible chapter of his record—a chapter dyed deep with blood.

At Darnall he was again the carver and gilder. But he had scarcely been in the place five minutes before he was made startingly aware of the fact that he had simply walked out of the frying-pan into the fire.

Almost the first name that met his eye as that of a prominent local resident was the name of Mr. Littlewood, an old prison chaplain he had met elsewhere under less favorable circumstances.

His presence of mind never failed him for a moment. Realizing that he would inevitably be recognized and his previous life made the talk of the village unless he took prompt action of some sort, he set his fertile brain to work, with the result that he decided on the bold course of an interview with his former priestly attendant.

The interview contains many amusing features which go to show the old lag's resourcefulness, to say nothing of a consummate impudence and more than a suspicion of native wit.

Walking up to the front door of the vicarage, attired in his Sunday best, he rang the bell. It was answered promptly by a neat servant girl, and Peace found himself ushered into Mr. Littlewood's well-furnished and comfortable study. Did he tremble or show the slightest sign of nervousness at the prospect of meeting again his old prison chaplain? We shall see.

The door opened. Mr. Littlewood stood on the threshold. With quick steps and every sign of affection and gratitude on his face, Peace walked up to him and seized the astonished man by the hand.

"Mr. Littlewood, sir," he commenced volubly. "What a treat this is to meet you again and to tell you how your wise counsels in the past have benefited me. Were it not for them I dread to think what might have become of me, whereas now you see before you a reformed character, the result of your ministrations. Mr. Littlewood, sir, did I not always say your words were like wine to me, giving me a new heart to try again?"

The worthy chaplain was quite taken off his feet. He passed his hand across his forehead before replying.

"But, Peace, if what you say is the truth, how comes it that you have been in prison again since the time when I visited you as chaplain?"

For a moment the ex-criminal was stumped, but only for a moment.

"That's true, sir," he said with great gravity, but still with full self-possession. "It was when I was in prison again that I thought most of your words. You see, you can't get real wine in prison."

And then he proceeded to follow up this sally by begging the clergyman to keep the secret of his past history from the remainder of the villagers.

Mr. Littlewood consented on condition that his former charge became a regular church-goer. The bargain was one after Peace's own heart. So well did the ex-burglar keep his word that very soon he was not only a regular attendant at church, but a teacher in the local Sunday school and altogether a model citizen—for the time.

We may well assume that at the beginning of his sojourn at Darnall Charles Peace did make a real effort to pull himself up and lead an honest life. But the task soon proved beyond his weight.

Never for one moment did the old Adam cease to torment him. His thoughts were forever straying off to matters connected with his former "trade," that should have been forgotten. His habits were those of a man accustomed by long training to a life of activity —doubtful activity. His fingers were itching to be at work again.

We may imagine him, if we will, seated in Mr. Littlewood's—his pastor's study, his mind torn between attending to the words of hope and comfort poured out for him by that good man and noting the interior arrangements of the room—just in case.

After a long wrestle with temptation he fell from grace The lapse was in itself a small one, but it marked the beginning of a resumption of his former evil ways.

The occasion was the annual school treat to the children. Hearing that there was to be an entertainment after the tea, it occurred to Peace that, as a "leading light" of the village, he ought to have some part in the festivities.

Now he happened to have in his possession a mechanical singing-bird. This he sent to the vicar with a note to the effect that he would be glad if he would allow an old friend to contribute towards the entertainment, and the bird was duly exhibited by Peace, to the infinite amusement of the children.

But the next morning the vicar missed the school clock!

In these matter-of-fact days there would probably be no two opinions as to the correct course to take under the circumstances. Darnall, however, was full of opinions. Nobody suspected the sanctimonious Sunday school teacher—except Mr. Littlewood!

Meeting his parishioner the next day, the vicar said quietly:

"Peace, you stole my clock!"

Never were there more passionate protestations of innocence. However, nothing was done, though it is said that one of the boys in the village positively identified Peace as the thief.

All the while that gentleman went about with an even countenance. One can imagine him taking an animated part in the discussion of the robberies. As the Sunday school teacher, he probably inspected the premises and tendered all sorts of expert advice on the subject. Such an adventure as this appealed to his sense of humor. In fact, the whole incident strikes one as a practical joke rather than as a crime. The old fox was simply frightening the chickens for the sake of enjoying the scare.

After a time Peace settled down to his old tricks. From Darnall he made many excursions to such places as Manchester, Liverpool, and Birmingham. All the plunder was sent home, where every now and then Peace went for rest and refreshment.

He usually did his business under an alias, so that though he was wanted in several places, the arm of the law was never able to reach him at Darnall, and he continued to live there without exciting the slightest suspicion.

But before proceeding further with the account of Charles Peace's history, there is a story in connection with the very mechanical singing bird alluded to above so strange that it must be recorded. The incident now to be related occurred while he was at Manchester.

He entered an inn one day, and immediately became, as was his wont, the life and soul of the party in the coffee-room. He turned the conversation on to musical instruments.

Suddenly putting his hand in his pocket he said:

"I have a curiosity here which may interest you."

The curiosity was the very mechanical singing bird, which he put on the table so that the company could hear it sing.

The performance had no sooner commenced than one of the men in the room went up to him and said:

"I beg your pardon, but there are only two of those birds in existence. Both were made by me. One I sold to a friend and the other was stolen. Do you mind telling me who you are?"

The predicament was awkward enough, but Peace wriggled out of it with the greatest ease. Winking at a friend who was with him, he affected great indignation that he should be asked such a question and at once strode out of the room.

"If you want to know who that is," said the friend when he had gone, "you had better go to Darnall and enquire for Mr. Charles Peace, of Darnall Hall."

The big name threw the enquirer off his guard and the subject was dropped.

As a matter of fact, Peace did at one time try to get a lease of the Hall. He offered a rental of fifty pounds a year. He said he wanted it as a store place.

So matters rubbed along till the latter part of 1875. Then something happened that, little as Peace suspected it, brought him all at once under the shadow of the gallows.

And yet the fatal circumstance was little enough in itself—no more, in fact, than the change of abode of a man, his wife, and his child.

Nor was it to be the first time that a trifling circumstance was to be fraught with the grimmest consequences.

CHAPTER VII.
The Murder of Mr. Dyson.

In the latter part of 1875 some people named Dyson moved into the house next to that occupied by the carver and gilder. Mr. Dyson was a retired engineer. He brought with him his wife—an accomplished and attractive woman. Unfortunately for her, she was just the kind of woman who appealed most to Peace.

The new neighbours were not long in making each other's acquaintance. The Dysons had some pictures to be framed, and Mrs. Dyson took them next door, where the work was executed to the lady's supreme satisfaction. Other commissions followed, and—what more natural?—Mr. Peace himself delivered the frames when finished.

After that he was a frequent visitor. At first Mr. Dyson had no objection to him; but after a time Peace developed the unpleasant habit of calling at all hours. Even when they were at their meals the Dysons discovered that they were by no means safe from his intrusions. Mr. Dyson decided this was too much of a good thing and took the following method of putting a stop to it.

He wrote on the back of one of his cards:

"*Charles Peace is requested not to interfere with my family,*" and threw the message into Peace's garden

Thereafter the carver and gilder was not admitted to the Dysons' house, but for all that he made himself a continual source of annoyance. He would loiter about the road and wait for Mrs. Dyson. Sometimes he was discovered listening at the keyhole of their door. Twice he dressed himself up as a woman and sought an interview with the object of his strange infatuation. He even followed them into an omnibus, so that he could sit opposite to them and make faces. Once he tried to trip Dyson up as he was walking along the street.

The climax came one evening when the demented husband seized Peace from behind as the latter was going into a public-house.

In a flash Peace turned like an eel, gripped the unfortunate engineer in a grip of iron, and shook him as if he were a child.

"What could I not do to you," he said, "if I were as cowardly?"

This tragic meeting had at least one good result. It made Mr. Dyson doubly cautious of his enemy, for it taught him that Peace possessed the strength of a giant.

But that night there was more trouble.

As Peace was walking along the street he heard Mrs. Dyson telling the neighbors about the incident of the afternoon.

Peace stopped in his walk and turned upon her.

"Are you talking about me?" he savagely demanded.

"Yes," she replied.

Peace angrily ordered her to repeat what she had said.

Mrs. Dyson repeated the conversation, whereupon Peace drew a revolver, and, pointing it at the woman, shouted:

"I'll blow your brains out and your husband's and all!"

A moment or two after this incident, which took place in the presence of several neighbours, the man had the impudence to say to another standing by:

"Now, Jim, you are witness that she struck me with that life preserver?"

"Jim" was incautious enough to point out that Mrs. Dyson had not even attempted to defend herself. To this, Peace replied that he had ammunition that would "do" for half a dozen of them. Then he muttered an oath and slouched sulkily away.

This was not all. For some time Peace had been carefully priming the people of Darnall with all sorts of criminal lies about the Dysons. These and other iniquities made the lives of his victims utterly unbearable, and Mr. Dyson at last determined to take steps to adequately protect his wife.

The morning after the assault and the threat a summons was issued against Peace, which that gentleman ignored. A few days afterwards, a warrant was out for his arrest, but when the officer went to Darnall to execute it he found that the bird had flown.

It has always been thought that Peace received secret warning of his danger. It may very well have been so, for throughout his career the burglar boasted that he never had any difficulty in acquainting himself with the plans laid by the police for his arrest. As we have seen, he certainly had some remarkable escapes.

For a time, then the carver and gilder was not at his business.

The Dysons soon had good reason to believe that their tormentor had taken refuge on the Continent, for they began to receive from him abusive letters stamped with the Hamburg postmark.

They might have known that Peace was not so far away.

He had simply handed the letters to a sea captain with instructions to post them abroad. The trick was completely sucessful.

To all intents and purposes, Peace had "left the country."

As a fact, where was he?

Let us see.

He first of all paid a short visit to Hull, but it was to Manchester that he ultimately fled from the warrant that was hanging over his head in Sheffield. Several burglaries were reported soon after his arrival—and then a mysterious murder took place.

On the night of August 1st, 1876, a police-constable named Cock was mortally wounded by a revolver-shot as he was attempting to arrest a suspicious character who was loitering about the ground surrounding the house of Mr. Gatrix at West Point, Whalley Range.

It was a dark night, and the murderer was not positively identified. But the Manchester police immediately arrested three brothers named Habron, one of whom was said to have threatened the dead constable a night or two before the murder.

After the usual police-court proceedings, two of the brothers,

THE LIFE STORY OF CHARLES PEACE

John and William, were tried and on November 29th John was acquitted and William was sentenced to death.

The trial excited tremendous interest. In spite of evidence that seemed to be overwhelming, the brothers protested their innocence unceasingly. Hundreds of people flocked to the court during the two days which the proceedings occupied. Amongst the spectators was one man who followed the trial in deadly earnest. He listened to the evidence word by word, he paid close attention to the speech for the defence and to the judge's summing-up; he heard the terrible sentence of death pronounced upon young William Harbon. Then he coolly left the court and had something to eat.

Yes, he can be described.

He was a little man, with a bald, retreating forehead.

He had deep-set, piercing eyes.

His nose was flat. His mouth was enormous.

He had a thick, swollen underlip and a powerful protruding jaw.

He was a small, lean, shrunken man, horribly ugly.

Next morning the same man turned up at the house of old Mrs. Peace in Sheffield, and, throwing a newspaper down on the table, said: "That's where I've been, mother."

* * * * * *

In the meantime he had boldly returned to Darnall on the understanding that there was no longer any danger.

But the Dysons were still apprehensive of him, so apprehensive that Mr. Dyson determined to remove his home to Banner Cross Terrace, Ecclesall, a village the other side of Sheffield.

On October 26th he sent his furniture in a wagon to the new home. He and his wife followed by rail. When they arrived, the first person they saw leaving the house in which the furniture was being placed was—Charles Peace.

Peace was the first to speak. He said to Mrs. Dyson:

"You see, I am here to annoy you wherever you go."

Mrs. Dyson reminded him that she had a warrant out for his apprehension, but the rascal replied that he didn't care for any warrant.

"I don't care for the police, either," he added with an oath.

For some days Peace was not seen again. As a matter of fact, he was "on business" in Manchester—and such business, too.

He was in Manchester on November 29th, the day of the trial of the Harbons.

More! His was the ugly face that was watching the proceedings from the gallery just as a hawk hovers over its prey.

* * * * * *

Now back to Sheffield—and Ecclesall.

It was still the evening of the 29th.

There came a knock at the door of Ecclesall Vicarage, and presently Mr. Charles Peace was ushered into the presence of the vicar, Mr. Newman.

A very significant visit this in view of that which the night was to bring forth. Peace began by telling the vicar all about his trials and temptations. Then he lapsed into a kind of confessional mood—his sins, his past life, his longing for forgiveness, and repentance. Had the parish priest been more of a student of human nature he might have humored his visitor's mood, the result of a refractory tortured brain. As is was, he let slip the golden opportunity to say those words of sympathy which might have saved Charles Peace from the gallows. Instead, he sat fidgeting in a bored and stony silence.

Suddenly the speaker's tune changed. He had come for human sympathy, and he had got none. The fire he had been trying to stifle flared up.

Now he raged about the wickedness of his neighbours; those Dysons especially—people not to be trusted! By-and-by, he lashed out into a regular fury of spite and aspersion.

And all the while the parson sat idly asking himself the question what this could possibly have to do with him, even assuming that it was all true. Presently he had listened to enough of it. Surely a parson is not bound to keep open house for every grumbler in the village? No, Mr. Charles Peace, it won't do.

The visitor was shown the door, and away he went straight as a die to Banner Cross.

Alas, Mr. Newman, you little dream what you have done to-night.

Peace is at Banner Cross Terrace now.

He asks a woman to go and tell Mrs. Dyson that an elderly gentleman is waiting for her. The woman refuses to take the message.

A moment later Mrs. Dyson goes into the garden with a lantern. As she is about to open the door of an outhouse she sees the face of the man she has come to dread staring at her out of the darkness.

"Speak! Say something!" demands Peace in a hoarse whisper; then as she stares at him tongue-tied, "Speak, or I'll fire!"

The startled woman screams.

At the same moment she sees in the gleam of the lantern the shining barrel of a revolver.

Alarmed by the scream, Mr. Dyson rushes into the garden to his wife's assistance. He sees the shadowy figure of a man hurrying off into the darkness. He follows.

The retreating form stops, turns, and fires.

The bullet is spattered against the wall.

A second shot is fired.

Mr. Dyson falls, mortally woulded.

In his study at the vicarage Mr. Newman, the clergyman, yawns once or twice as he begins to think about turning into bed. He has had a long day and a tiring one, but it has been a good, a useful day as well.

THE LIFE STORY OF CHARLES PEACE 43

As he stretches out his hand for the candle that is to light him to his cosy bed he even heaves a little satisfied sigh and quotes to himself the well-worn couplet:

Something attempted, something done,
Has earned a night's repose.

If he could know what he had done!

CHAPTER VIII.

The Murderer Hunt Commences.

* * * * * *

MURDER

One hundred Pounds Reward.

WHEREAS on the 29th ult. Mr. Albert Dyson, C. E., was murdered at Banner Cross, Sheffield, having been shot in the head in the presence of his wife by Charles Peace, who escaped in the darkness of the night, and is still at large, and WHEREAS at the coroner's inquest, held on the 5th inst. upon the body of the said Albert Dyson, a verdict of wilful murder was found against the said Charles Peace, NOTICE is hereby given that a reward of one hundred pounds will be paid by Her Majesty's Government to any person other than a person employed in a police-office in the United Kingdom who shall give such information and evidence as will lead to the discovery and conviction of the said Charles Peace.

* * * * * *

Great as was the sentation caused by the Banner Cross murder, it was as nothing compared to the excitement which was aroused by the disclosures which followed it.

At first the crime was regarded as of no more than local importance. But as soon as the name of the criminal was public property astonishing details of Peace's past life literally poured into Sheffield.

In less than a week the whole country was on the track of a man whom it was known was perhaps the master criminal of the day.

The supreme difficulty in the case was not to find evidence, but to sort out from the mass of detail that almost overwhelmed the police something that was likely to lead to the capture of Mr. Dyson's murderer.

The Banner Cross affair was followed by all the strange tricks and turns that are just as much features of crime investigation today as they were thirty years ago.

North, south, east and west—one man after another gave himself up for the murder of Mr. Dyson. On scores of occasions "Peace" was "seen" and "spoken" to either by old associates or by people who said they recognized him from the description that had been issued by the police. Suspect after suspect was detained. A constable even arrested a harmless Frenchman who could hardly speak a word of English.

But the public mind had been so primed with fantastic details of Peace's character and habits that it was over and over again declared that "at last" the murderer had been captured and was on his way to Sheffield.

In Darnall the unrest took a more alarming phase.

There, it was believed that Peace would return in the dead of night and wreak a terrible vengeance on his "calumniators." People refused to leave their houses at night. Some there were who believed that their late neighbour had committed suicide. Every pool and river near the village was carefully searched.

The police might have known their man better than that. As a matter of fact, one or two shrewd officers were already on his track. But no details of the pursuit leaked out—only a wierd succession of tales. And such tales!

The appearance of Peace at this time can be gathered from the following graphic description of him, which was issued immediately after the murder:—

CHARLES PEACE. *Wanted for murder on the night of the 29th ult. He is thin and slightly built, from fifty-five to sixty years of age, five feet four inches or five feet high, grey (nearly white) hair, beard, and whiskers. His whiskers were long when he committed the murder, but may now be cut or shaved off. He lacks one or more fingers off the left hand, walks with his legs rather wide apart, speaks somewhat peculiarly as though his tongue was too large for his mouth, and is a great boaster. He is a picture-frame maker. He occasionally cleans and repairs clocks and watches and sometimes deals in oleographs, engravings, and pictures. He has been in penal servitude for burglary in Manchester. He has lived in Manchester, Salford, Liverpool, and Hull.*

A few days after that description had been published it was supplemented by the following additional details:—

Alias *George Parker, Alexander Mann, "Paganini." Age, forty-six. He looks ten years older.*

Then the Government offered the reward of a hundred pounds already set forth, for his capture, and henceforth Charles Peace, outlawed and hunted, was fighting the terrible battle of the fugutive against society.

From this time his life is one of unceasing vigilance. Night and day, waking and sleeping, there is no rest for him. Wherever he goes he is "wanted."

And, although he cannot even see the fringe of it, yet the net is closing in.

* * * * * *

After the murder Charles Peace absolutely disappeared.
What had become of him?

THE LIFE STORY OF CHARLES PEACE

It is the man himself who shall tell us what he did after his flight from Banner Cross with the ghost of Albert Dyson haunting him as he hurried across the dark fields to Sheffield.

"From the very moment that I left Banner Cross on November 29th 1876, I had no fear of being taken prisoner, knowing that I had done nothing wrong. When it happened, I came down the passage and stood in the middle of the road, not knowing what had happened. I did not know whether to run away or to walk away till I heard Kate scream, and then, knowing what had happened, I took across the road and fields to Encliffe Crescent. I afterwards went to see my mother, and remained with her for more than half an hour. I went to see my wife and family at 27 Collier Street, the next morning."

Late at night, then, he reached Sheffield, a travel-stained dishevelled fugitive.

His face was ghastly white. His eyes, always strangely wild, were now aglow with the flames kindled by knowledge of pressing danger.

On the outskirts of the town he paused. Whither should he go? Who in all that crowded city would give him shelter even for an hour? His friends—his mother?

Ah, yes. There was his mother.

He must be quick. The Sheffield police would know soon.

At last he stood breathless at her door.

Should he enter? Yes.

He lifted the latch. A moment more, and his mother, seeing him and noting his wild, hunted look, knew her boy was in danger. She uttered a choking cry.

"Don't mother!" he implored. "Don't be frightened. It's done, and it can't be helped. I've been and shot Dyson!"

At first it seemed as if the woman was going to swoon.

The shock to her was almost as much as she could bear, for all the previous bad bringing-up of her son. Afterwards she asked for an explanation, and he told this story:

"I went up to see Mrs. Dyson. While I was there he—Mr. Dyson—came up and took hold of me, and we had a struggle. He had a warrant out against me, and I did not want to be took, as I knew my past life would go against me."

A moment later he added:

"I do not know that I have killed him, but I shot him to get away, and"—he pulled out a revolver—"I did it with this!"

There was a scream, and Peace turned away.

He hurried upstairs to change his clothes.

A bright clear night; in the air just that invigorating touch that one sometimes, though rarely, feels at all time of the year. Just the sort of night for a brisk walk under the stars.

A shambling figure, with great-coat-collar turned up close about the face, walked furtively into the railway station and asked for a ticket for Hull.

The ticket was issued; then followed a long, terribly long, and anxious wait till the train should arrive.

Thank goodness! Here it comes at last around the bend of the line, and seeming to swell before one's eyes as it approached nearer and nearer to the station.

It was in the station, and almost at a standstill.

The wizened, cloaked figure darted one ferret-like glance in the direction of the station entrance to make sure he was not being followed, then sprang for a carriage and took his place inside.

It was Charles Peace. He was going to try and obtain shelter under the roof of Hannah Peace, who was still keeping a provision shop at the town whither he had booked.

Smack! Clap! Bang! One after another the carriage doors were being shut. Peace heard the lazy porter stumping down the platform as he performed his noisy duty, and his heart rose within him.

Each slam of the door meant one more chance of freedom.

Now they were all shut. The guard gave one last survey of the train ere he put his whistle to his lips and blew a shrill double blast, the signal to the driver to start.

Toot! Toot!

Shriek!

Off at last. The fugitive heaved a sigh of relief.

At the booking-office a stalwart, heavily-built man, his feet encased in extraordinarily large boots, fumed as he held out his hand for the ticket that never seemed to come.

Hark! The whistle had gone. He would miss his train unless he liked to dash for it without a ticket.

Ah, yes; that was what he would do. The matter was urgent. No; no need after all. Here was the ticket at last.

Now to make a run for it. Already the engine had given its first cough; the white steam was swirling out of the funnel. The carriages had made their first lurch forward, and were rapidly gathering impetus.

"Your change, sir," called the clerk, as the big man ran wildly from the booking-office.

Change? Never mind that. Never mind anything so long as the train was caught.

He was out on the platform now and racing madly after the rear carriage as it whirled out of the station.

A leap for the footboard.

"Stand away there!" shouts the porter, and after him the station-master, "Stand away!"

They try to drag the passenger from the opening carriage-door, but he is too quick.

THE LIFE STORY OF CHARLES PEACE

He clambered inside now and slammed it behind him. The train has been caught after all. A narrow shave, though.

Thus Police-constable Pearson started on his journey to Hull to watch and search the eating-house kept by Hannah Ward—or Peace—in the hope that the murderer would do the very thing he was doing, that he would go there for hiding from the sleuth-hounds of the law.

If only Police-constable Pearson could have told who was at that very moment sitting in a corner of another compartment of the same train!

CHAPTER IX.

Peace the Wanderer.

Arrived at Hull, the police-officer first made his way to the police head-quarters to report and arrange matters in the event of an arrest being effected.

Meanwhile Charles Peace took himself straight to the little restaurant, where, after explaining the reasons for his secrecy and warning his female confederate to keep a strict look-out for police-officers, he sat himself down in the back parlour to the enjoyment of a quiet bowl of soup.

Not very long afterwards Constable Pearson arrived on the scene. Threading his way through innumerable mean streets, full of criminals and semi-criminals, he at length came to the eating-house and peered cautiously in at the door.

Careful as he thought he was, he was not careful enough to elude the eye of the watchful Hannah.

Quickly by a single whispered word she gave her master "the office."

Suddenly Peace put down his soup and crept away like a weasel. Not even a board creaked as he made his esape.

The unsuspecting police-officer opened the shop door and walked inside. At the sound of footsteps the woman turned. Her face was bruised and broken. She had two black eyes.

"Where's Charlie?" asked the detective.

"I don't know" the woman wearily replied. "I haven't seen him for a long time."

Then she pointed to her swollen face.

"This is what he did when he was home last. I only wish you could find him. He beat me something shocking!"

What a change had come over the woman since we first met her on the canal bank years ago.

The constable searched the house from floor to roof. He could find nothing. He bade Mrs. Peace "Good-Night." He was going back to Sheffield, so he said.

*   *   *   *   *   *

But the wily constable did not go back to Sheffield. We know it was not without reason that he had searched the little eating-house. Charles Peace was in Hull somewhere. He felt convinced of it. But where?

He waited on in the town for some days in the hope of something turning up to re-mould his convictions into certainties.

And then the thing he had been waiting for occurred.

On February 10th, 1877, Mr. C. E. Johnson, of Lister Street, Hull, was shot at as he was pursuing a burglar whom he had discovered trying to enter his premises.

Shortly afterwards a tavern was robbed of two pounds in money and fifteen pounds' worth of cigars. A watch-dog in the yard was drugged.

The constable waited no longer.

Accompanied by several Hull detectives, he swooped down on the ham shop one night. They found nothing—only Mrs. Peace. She was very flurried. The officers wondered why.

An explanation was forthcoming in the morning.

A woman who lived about two hundred yards from the shop reported that on the previous evening a man had scrambled through her garret window. He threatened her with death if she screamed. She therefore allowed him to remain for a couple of hours, when after looking carefully up and down the street, he went away.

The police at once examined Mrs. Ward's house. They found that a man of Pearce's agility could easily get out on to the roof by the top bedroom window and crawl along on the tiles to the house he was believed to have taken refuge.

Once again the master criminal had come to grips with the might of the English law, and once again he had emerged from the conflict victorious.

Hull was ransacked in vain for the fugitive. Every low street and alley was searched over inch by inch. All to no avail. Peace had suddenly vanished into thin air, so the searchers must have thought. As a matter of fact, where was he. He was quietly cooling his heels in some lodgings near the—Police Station.

Could anything have been more characteristic of the man? Day after day he watched the hurried comings and goings a few doors away. He even stood by whilst the zealous Pearson was putting up the bill describing his appearance.

When it was nicely pasted on to the board Peace read it through.

"Grey (nearly white) hair, beard, and whiskers."

Unconsciously Peace's hand went up to his beard as he stood in the street reading.

"Grey beard and whiskers." That would never do!

He promptly went indoors and shaved.

After he had been in Hull for three weeks, Peace decided that to remain any longer in a neighbourhood with which he was known to be associated would be too serious a tax even on his infinite powers of disguise and impersonation.

The Banner Cross murderer himself shall tell the story of his wanderings that immediately followed.

"I left Hull," he says, "and booked from Doncaster to London. I then went to Bristol, which was the first place I saw a reward out for my apprehension. Next I booked from Bristol to Bath. I stopped at Bath all night, booked from Bath to Oxford.

"In the carriage with me there was a police-sargeant on his way to Stafford Assizes. We rode and talked together to Didcot Junction and arrived there in the middle of the night. We slept together in the waiting-room for about four hours, and then went forward to Oxford by a fast train. We then shook hands and parted. I remained at Oxford all day."

What a situation!

"We rode and talked together." Talked about the murder, and wondered when that ruffian Peace would be captured.

And all the time there was that left hand with the missing fingers. Could there be a more startling illustration of the man's wierd contempt for the police? He used to say, "A policemtn always goes by the face. He never thinks of looking at people's hands."

And over and over again Peace proved the truth of his axiom. It is true that he had recourse to all sorts of disguises. He nearly always wore black gloves. There were fingers on the left-hand glove stuffed so as to correspond with those that were missing.

Day and night he carried about with him the gutta-percha dummy fitted with the hook, so that at any moment he could turn himself into a one-armed man. As for his face, he had such control over the muscles that his features were as pliable as wax.

By these means he was able to live in Hull undetected; he was able to hold peaceful converse with the policeman in the train.

And always the hundred pounds waited for anyone who could beat Peace at his own game.

In all England there was not a soul worthy of the challenge.

Fresh from his adventure with the policeman, Peace descended upon Birmingham, and then went to Derby, where, in order to be absolutely safe from detection, he adopted his favorite plan of living as near the police-station as possible. He watched the policemen going in and out of the station, and even spoke to those whom his instinct told him he could trust.

But most astounding of all as an illustration of his daring comes the story of how he revisited the scene of the Banner Cross murder.

Probably it is true that he did so. He declared it with great solemnity. Moreover, it is a well-known fact that criminals are constantly led by a sort of morbid attraction to visit the scene of their crimes.

So much is said of them by criminologists, as if criminals thereby showed themselves to be different from the ordinary run of humanity. As a matter of fact, this is not so. Do not all people show this same tendency to revisit the scenes of their strongest emotions?

Do not couples usually make the celebration of their silver wedding the occasion for revisiting the scenes of their courtship and marriage? Does not the millionaire make a special trip late in life to view again the humble cottage where life commenced? Then what wonder if a criminal should do the same? What wonder that he should feel irresistably drawn to the spot where took place the strangest, most awful act of his career?

We may take it, then, for certain that Charles Peace did revisit the scene of his crime.

What wierd terror lies in the thought!

A lonely country road leading up to a terrace of small detached houses standing in their own gardens. Round about the rustle of dead twigs as the tree tops sigh in the swirl of the wind.

Overhead the dull drap of a drizzling sky, with, far away to the west, a single hard grey jab, like the rent in a ragged coat, through which the moonbeams try in vain to escape.

For the rest, gloom. In the gloom, a man. He is peering over the wooden railings of one of the houses, gazing in at the garden with fascination in his terror-haunted eyes. It is Charles Peace, the fugitive—returned.

As he stares, a shutter flaps before one of the dark windows. He starts and cries out as if he had been struck. For once in his life his iron nerve has deserted him.

A bat bumps against the notice-board in the garden announcing the house to let—the house of ill-omen that no one will take—and once again Peace flinches and a dry gurgle rises in his throat.

And then it is as though into the darkness comes a faint beam of light. It is low down, close to the ground, flickering now and growing brighter moment by moment like a candle or—or—

Good heavens! it is a stable lantern, and by the side of it kneels the fiugre of a woman, supporting on her lap the head of a murdered man. Peace tries to call for help, but no sound will come. He is trembling, so that he has to clutch at the slime-covered railings for support.

And then the phantom figure of the murdered Dyson raises his head and looks at his murderer—such a look.

With a stifled shriek the wretched man staggers away, pursued by a thousand howling demons, the victims of a guilty conscience.

CHAPTER X.

The Meeting with the Traitress Sue.

From Banner Cross Peace went to Derby, and from thence to Nottingham, where something happened that was destined to play a strange part in his career.

He did not know it, but the net was being drawn still closer in.

The particular thing that happened was his forming the acquaintance of Sue Thompson, of Nottingham, the woman who eventually informed on him to the police.

The girl was a native of the city in which Peace met her. Her maiden name was Susan Grey. At the age of twenty-four she married a man named Bailey. After her marriage she went to reside with her sister in Nottingham till the year 1877, the year in which she became acquainted with Peace.

The fugitive was then lodging with a Mrs. Anderson, a buyer, next door to the Woodman Inn, in Narrow Marsh. In the same house the girl was fighting hard for her living.

The famous Sue is described as possessing a German cast of feature. She had light brown eyes and a profusion of fair hair. She was somewhat above the height of the average woman, and she had besides a distinctly superior manner.

It is to be feared that among the Banner Cross murder's numerous failings must be numbered a certain laxity of moral calibre, for, whatever position Hannah Ward may have occupied in the household up to now, we have to follow Peace and Sue to London in the character of Mr. and Mrs. Thompson.

The metropolis then received them as it always has and always will receive the dregs as well as the flower of society. Three weeks after the couple bade farewell to Mrs. Adamson and her hospitality they were to all intents and purposes lost in the "hub of the universe." But previous to that many little affairs had happened chiefly of interest to Peace on account of the gain involved to him, and to the public on account of the loss entailed to it. As it happens, the burglar has himself a record of the events occurring in that interval—a record written up in his own words. It forms in itself a striking narrative, none the less so because set forth in Peace's own phraseology and because presumably, true. As we have already pointed out, so far as we can be judged, the confessions made from time to time by Charles Peace seem uniformly to bear the light of verification.

"Upon one occasion," he says, "I booked from Nottingham to Sheffield, but got out of the train at Heeley Station, and walked past the police-station at Highfields—Inspector Bradbury stood at the police-station door—at about seven o'clock at night. I passed close by him, and he did not know me then.

"I went right away up to Sharrow and crossed over quite close to Banner Cross and down into Eccleshall Road, turned down towards Sheffield and crossed through Broomhall Park into Havelock Square. I that night did a house over at the corner of Havelock Square. They were away from home. I got about six pounds in money and a lot of jewellery. The watchman on the beat fancied he heard something in the house. But I saw him stop the sergeant when he came his round, and I got away backwards. I went to Heeley Railway Station, and from Heeley to Nottingham. At Nottingham I done a big tailor and draper establishment for a lot of overcoats and cloth. I think it is in Castlegate.

I then done a very big mantle place in Derby for a number of women's mantels and money. It was the Burton Road end. I then went back to Nottingham and done a great many gentlemen's houses. I then went to Melton Mowbray to a lord's house and brought away a great quantity of valuable jewels and plate. I then went back to Nottingham.

"Me and Mrs. Thompson then went to live at a policeman's house. It was in a street at the back of Sanger's Circus of Anlaby Road, opposite a chapel. We lived there from three weeks to a month. I went to Leicester and brought some plate home. I then went back to Nottingham and worked as before. Me and Mrs. Thompson then went down to Hull for a week. We then went back to Nottinghom, and I did a large silk robbery in the market-place, next to the new post-office." A modest story this, full of thrilling episode.

For the first six weeks after the arrival of Peace and Sue Thompson in town they lived at Royal Street, Lambeth. Peace had now to consider not only Hannah Ward, who was still at Hull, but also his new-found accomplice.

It looks as if he had decided to confine his attentions exclusively to the South of England, for immediately after his arrival in London, he determined to close the shop in Hull, and to have Mrs. Ward under his own eys. But the thing was easier said than done. Hannah was not at all anxious to leave the cook-shop.

Again and again Peace wrote, asking the woman to come up to London. Mrs Ward paid no attention to his entreaties, so at last the rascal had recourse to a trick.

One day a worried and dishevelled-looking woman presented herself at the counter of the eating-house. After looking around carefully to make sure that no one was observing her, she took from beneath her shawl a greasy letter, which she handed to Mrs. Ward.

The letter turned out to be a more than ever alluring request to go to London. Peace informed her that out of regard for her fidelity he had bought her a business in Tottenham Court Road, where she would be able to live in comfort with her son for the rest of her days.

In less than a week poor Hannah called at Stangate Street, Lambeth, where the first woman she saw was the dishevelled creature who had handed her the letter in Hull—Sue Thompson.

As soon as she realized she had been successfully tricked, she undoubtedly accepted the new conditions without a murmur.

She was accompanied to town by her son Willie, the child of the canal bank, now a young man.

From that time onward till his arrest Peace occupied the same house as the two women, though as far as his intimacy with Sue Thompson was concerned, it seems to have been one long succession

THE LIFE STORY OF CHARLES PEACE

of quarrels, a state of things by no means bettered by the fact of the woman's increasing addiction to drink.

For all that, it was some time before Sue discovered that the man she was living with was the notorious Banner Cross murderer. The revelation came about in this way:

She was turning over some things one day when she came across a memorial notice relating to the members of his family, which Peace had intended should be inscribed on a monument of his own design when the proper time arrived.

Amongst the names was that of "Charles Peace."

Terrified beyond measure, she rummaged amongst the rest of his belongings and found a packet of letters which proved, without a doubt, Peace's connection with the murder at Banner Cross.

What took place between the two when these discoveries were reported no one knows.

This much is certain: She destroyed every incriminating document she could find, but Peace always regarded her with suspicion. He know that she drank, and he was always fearful lest in a drunken bout she should blurt out the secret of the respectable old gentleman who was known as her husband.

How far more than justified were these fears of his will appear later. Meanwhile Peace decided upon a change of abode.

After a family consultation it was decided that the headquarters should be moved to Greenwich, where Peace took two houses next door to each other for the accommodation f his family.

He let the neighbors understand that he was a gentleman of independent means, and, as most people in London are "something in the City," Peace, who was at home all day, easily maintained the deception.

There now took place a noticeable change in Peace's mode of life which suggests that he was no longer haunted by memories of Banner Cross, and was growing bolder. He was no longer the tramp or the out-of-work sailor living in cheap doss-houses. Landladies and lodging-houses knew him no more. He dressed well and wore expensive jewellery. He affected a nice taste in coloured waistcoats and bright ties He always had plenty of money to spend, and he entertained generously as became a gentleman of his position.

One small house was not good enough for him. He told the Greenwich landlord that he wanted plenty of accommodation. Consequently he bargained for the two houses side by side.

He soon became popular as a sort of Greenwich character. His frineds called him Captain Johnson by way of tribute to his enviable circumstances. So much for his doings during the daytime.

At night "business" went on as usual.

Greenwich turned out to be a splendid hunting-ground. Scattered around him for miles were thousanads of houses, most of them having in front those ornamental porticos, which are so convenient for "gentlemen" who wish to call without invitation.

There is no complete record of his doings at this time. After his capture hundreds of robberies were put down to him, but with many of them he had nothing to do.

But it was at Peckham, where he went in May of 1877, that he eclipsed himself and rose to heights of daring from which he was so soon to fall.

CHAPTER XI.

The Home at Peckham.

The new home was at 5, East Terrace, Evelina Road. For the benefit of his landlady he repeated the tales about his position with which he had blinded the neighbors at Greenwich, and the new tenant was received as a highly desirable ornament of a locality which, in those days, was not without pretensions.

From May, 1877, to October, 1878, was the most fascinating period of Peace's career. In those months are gathered all the lessons that Peace had learned during his strange journey through life. We come, as it were, into closer touch with him. To a certain extent the highwayman and the outlaw recede into the background, and there remains behind the little old gentlemtn who might have been anything from a great comedian to a successful engineer.

It is at Peckham that we find Peace engaged on his inventions together with his friend Mr. Brion, of whom more will be said later. Here also he gave full rein to his liking for animals.

It has always been pointed out as one proof of the theory that Peace's life was dominated by some strange twist in his character, for which he could not be held responsible, that he was devoted to animals.

That his nature was so full of contradictions is very strong evidence of a constitutional warp. The man who would shoot human beings without compunction when his own skin was at stake often said that to hurt even a mouse was beyond him. He even went so far as to declare that if he had to kill his own meat he would abstain from animal food for the rest of his life.

It is true that he had whilst he lived at Peckham a collection of pets by which he set great store. It consisted of a number of pigeons, rabbits, guinea pigs, and other domestic animals which Peace never tired of showing to his friends. Indeed, it has been suggested that he kept the creatutres so that he could have an excuse for inviting the neighbors to the house. In the face of the thousand and one other excuses Peace's fertile brain could have made up, had the man wished—all of them far less expensive than the keeping of live pets—this latter theory would not seem to bear serious consideration.

Another pet was the famous pony "Tommy." Had "Tommy" been endowed with speech he could have told many strange tales about Peace's doings, for he and his master shared many an adventure of which nothing will probably ever be heard.

"Tommy." like his master, was an oddity in his way. At the word of command he would rear himself up on his hind legs and remain in that position until another word of command released him. Or he would lie down and pretend to be dead. He was also credited with knowing his master's mind so thoroughly that he understood a special code of signals which enabled Peace to dispense with the more or less noisy sounds which are used whilst driving.

Peace had also wonderful control over dogs. Several he had were important featutres of his backyard collection.

So thoroughly did he understand the canine race that he was supposed to be able with a look or a word to reduce the fiercest watchdog to submission. As a matter of fact, in nearly every instance in which he was confronted by a dog whilst he was at "work," he either shot, poisoned, or drugged it—usually the latter. Still, it was useful to be regarded as a sort of mesmerist, and Peace assiduously cultivated those rumors whenever he came across them.

Whilst he was out with "Tommy" he certainly had one adventure which might have cost him dear but for the astonishing fact that he was able to go about in broad daylight absolutely undetected.

On Whit Monday he was taking a party of friends out for a drive when he crashed into a butcher's cart and badly damaged it.

As Peace was in the wrong, the proper thing to do under the circumstances was to at least say something by way of apology. Not he. He jumped to the ground and poured out such a volley of abuse on the unfortunate butcher that that individual at once summoned a policeman.

Here, indeed, was a dilemma. A man with a price of a hundred pounds on his head arguing with a policeman. Peace took the situation in hand and dealt with it boldly.

When the constable asked him what his name was, he replied, "John Thompson, of Greenwich." And then, as an afterthought, he quietly added, "You can put Esquire, if you like."

"Tommy" was once responsible for another risky meeting between the Banner Cross murderer and the police.

It happened that one night Peace drove his pony so furiously into the stable at Peckham that the gate was knocked down. The noise attracted the attention of a police-consable, who walked up to the shed, where, by the light of a lantern, he saw that Mr. Thompson looked very much as if he had just reached home after a long journey of extraordinary haste. Peace wasa taking the harness off the pony when he caught the eye of the constable. Once more his wonderful wits came to the rescue.

Although it was one o'clock in the morning, he invited the constable into the stable. Pointing to a tin box, he said:

HE INVITED THE CONSTABLE INTO THE STABLE

"I've just came back from some important experiments with an invention Mr. Brion and I are patenting, and you know it wouldn't do to let people know about this in the daytime."

A bottle of beer was then produced, and the constable drank to the success of the invention, after which he assisted in replacing the gate upon its hinges.

There can be no doubt that Peace had just returned from one of his nocturnal expeditions. But what would have happened to the constable if he had been sagacious enough to make more inquiries it is not easy to surmise.

From this it will be seen that the pony played a prominent part in many of Peace's later adventures.

After his identification as the murderer of Mr. Dyson, and especially after sentence of death had been passed on him, stories of "Tommy" formed a main subject of converse between him and the warders who were told off to watch him. He never seemed to weary of recounting incidents in the life of his favourinte animal.

One story in particular which bears the hall-mark of truth stands out from the rest to show beyond a doubt how deeply was hiis affection for his four-footed friend.

Peace had brought off a haul at a country house in Surrey and was returning with the spoils in his cart. It was the depth of winter, and recent floods had rendered the low-lying moorland over which he had to traverse, exceptionally boggy and dangerous.

To make matters worse, the night was pitch dark and the road—which he had chosen as an unfrequented short cut—almost unknown to him.

"Tommy" had been plodding on for more than an hour through the drenching rain—both he and his master were long ago soaked to the skin—when Peace felt one of the wheels of the cart sink beneath him.

In vain he drew in the reins in an effort to pull up on the edge of the morass. The action only reared the pony on his hind legs, with the result that they sank into the treacherous bog almost to the hocks. At the same time the other wheel began slowly, but surely, to subside.

What was to be done? By now the poor beast was kicking and plunging frantically, while each maddened effort at escape from the wet mud that sucked it down only made matters worse and worse. Deeper and deeper it was sinking. It seemed as if, whatever chance there might be of the flat-bottomed cart remaining above the surface of the quagmire, "Tommy" was doomed.

And then Peace did a thing few other men would have done under the circumstances. Deliberately forsaking the comparative safety afforded by the trap, he flung himself out on to the quaking turf, still clutching the reins as he went.

He was out now among the treacherous green reeds, which, had there been light in the sky, would have warned him beforehand of the danger into which he was driving. Already, as he struggled to the pony's head he could feel his feet being sucked down deeper and deeper.

It was as much as he could do to raise his legs at all. One or two more last successful attempts and the effort became futile. He was sinking just as surely as was his dumb friend. But now he was at the pony's head, with his hand on its tossing forehead caressing and soothing it. At any rate, if "Tommy" must go, then he would not buy his life at the expense of weighting the cart, and so lessening whatever microscopical chanace the pony might have of coming out of the adventure unscathed.

Peace was down to his waist now, but, thanks to his restraining hand, the pony was keeping quiet. Moreover, the shafts seemed to be preventing it from sinking further.

A few more inches of welling mud rising about the burglar's body, and then—

Peace felt something under his feet. At first he could scarcely believe his senses, yet another moment or two and the happy truth was made all to plain.

The quagmire, such as it was, was in reality a shallow affair, the result of the heavy deluge of the past months. He was actually standing on firm ground.

A few minutes of struggling, and he succeeded in pushing his way up on to dry land once more, still holding the reins in a firm grasp.

Then, last of all, the pony was drawn by their means to safety.

The task was long and arduous, nor was it accomplished until both the burglar and his favourite animal were reduced to the last stage of exhaustion. That it was accomplished at all may be looked upon as entirely due to Peace's self-sacrifice.

As to the valuables stowed awaya in sacks in the cart, they were pitched out into the morass, and disappeared for good long before the cart itself was dragged into safety.

If only the exact position of the former quagmire could be ascertained it might be worth while even now after all the lapse of years to seek out and dig down for the engulfed treasure. Unfortunately the warders who heard the tale never thought of putting such questions as would have elicited its whereabouts at a time when the one who alone could have enlightened them was still living.

It is, however, interesting to note in this connection that shortly after this incident must have taken place—somewhere about the December or January of 1877—a school child playing on a Surrey common picked up and brought home to its mother a piece of paper. Scribbled over it were what appeared to be a mixture of cabalistic signs and meaningless words.

At the time little or nothing was thought of the find, though a local schoolmaster, who chanced to see the paper, confessed to certain

THE LIFE STORY OF CHARLES PEACE

suspicions that it was a cipher message of some sort. However, the paper was destroyed, and so far there is an end of it.

For all that, it is highly probable, in face of the subsequent discoverry of Charles Peace's secret code and alphabet, that the paper so lightly thrown aside might, if kept, have proved the key to the present resting place of the cartload of valuables.

* * * * * *

Meanwhile the fool's paradise at Evelina Road, Peckham was playing its strange part in the career of its lord and master. Concerts, tea-parties, and social gatherings—these were the order of the day.

The house is said to have been luxuriously furnished. As a matter of fact, its contents were of the kind—with a few notable exceptions—which one would expect to see in the neighborhood. There was a dining-room suite covered with red plush, a harmonium, some violins, and a picture or two. The ornaments would probably have attracted one's attention most. They had obviously come from more cultivated surroundings. In another room there was a piano. Peace, in fact, was engaged in the important operating of furnishing. A great many wild tales have been circulated to the effect that he used to carry away heavy pieces of furniture wholesale. That may have been so. Very little of it found its way to Evelina Road. Peace used to store things in empty houses taken for the purpose. At the time of his arrest there was one stuffed quite full of tables, chairs, and other objects.

Outside, the most noticeable thing about the place was the substantial fence that entirely closed in the back garden and screened it from the gaze of inquisitive neighbors. Peace put this fence up himself. One day a neighbour found him, hammer in hand, working like a nigger. Noticing that Peace was using a wood rather more expensive than was usually applied to such a job, he asked why a little more though was not expended on economy.

"Well, it's this way," replied Peace. "I'm working at an invention that may be very valuable, and it wouldn't do to have people watching me, so I'm putting up a good fence."

He was just as particular about a bit of shed he put up for the accommodation of the pony and trap. No uninvited eye ever pierced the secret of that shed, though the neighbors could sometimes hear sounds of feverish toil in it even to the small hours of the morning.

But then Mr. Thompson was such a claver man. His little peculiarities were easily explained.

It was a noisy household. When its inmates were not quarrelling they were droning out hymns on the wheezy harmonium. Peace had a nice taste in hymns. The neighbors could always tell when "dear old Mr. Thompson" was playing, for he would have Moody and Sanky or nothing at all—a fact which considerably raised him in the good graces of the road.

One day was very much like another. As Mr. Thompson was "very delicate," his good wife never allowed him to leave his bed till the middle of the day. As soon as he got down there was generally a bit of work to be done in the shed. Well, indeed, for Peace that the neighbours could not see what he was about. It would have been very awkward, for example, if they had seen poor "Tommy" weary, bedraggled, and bespattered with mud.

They could, of course, hear the clattering that went on in the small, wee hours when "Tommy" and sometimes as many as two passengers returned to the shed. That was easily accounted for. Mr. Thompson "suffered from insomnia," and the doctor thought a drive at night would bring sleep to the old eyes. Little did they know.

Sometimes he went to the public house close by. He was always welcome. The old gentleman with plenty of money was a boon companion, for he often ordered drinks all round. But no matter how many drinks he paid for Mr. Thompson never took more than one. If he stood two rounds, his first drink was still unconsumed when the others were drinking their second. Even when they were drinking their third and their fourth glass there was still a drain in Mr. Thompson's.

Yes, it was strange; but as the old fellow was reputed to have plenty of money no one thought of asking questions. Mr. Thompson's abstemiousness was simply regarded as one more virtue.

On his walk home again he made a practice of distributing sixpences to children he met by the way. "Dear, soft-hearted Mr. Thompson!"

And what good company he was to be sure. He could tell such funny tales. Or, if you went to Evelina Road, he could sing you such a merry ditty that the music-halls were not in it.

Two or three times in the week Mrs. Thompson was at home to her friends. On these occasions Mr. Thompson would take his place at the tea-table. He always wore a skull-cap, in which he looked the very essence of sanctity. The tea-cups would rattle away for an hour or so, and then the room would be cleared for music. Peace had not forgotten the tuition he received from his father in his early days, and both he and Willie were tolerable performers. All would go as merry as a marriage-bell till about eight o'clock.

About that hour the host would quietly rise from his seat. This was regarded as a hint to the company that the evening's entertainment was at an end. Mrs. Thompson always explained to strangers that her husband was in the habit of retiring early. What could have been more reasonabale Mr. Thompson was "getting on." He wanted rest.

That was Mr. Thompson as his neighbors saw him. As to the real reason why the man wanted his nights to himself we can probably guess.

THE LIFE STORY OF CHARLES PEACE

CHAPTER XII.

A Burglary or So.

All the time he was robbing and pillaging north, south, east, and west of London, till, by October, 1878, the police had evidence of something like twenty-six burglaries which were afterwards traced to him, to say nothing of dozens of others which were never brought home to him at all.

He plundered at Portsmouth, Southsea, and Southampton. He broke into Lord Shaftsbury's place at Wandsworth. Honor Oak, Blackheath, Streatham, Herne Hill, and Brixton all paid toll to him.

He even paid another visit to Hull, as the following letter—written after Peace's final capture—to the Chief Constable from the late Sir Howard Vincent, then Director of the Criminal Investigation Department, which he had recently founded at Scotland Yard shows:—

Sir,—With reference to John Ward, alias Peace, a convict undergoing the sentence of penal servitude for life, it may interest you to know that he alleges that early in the year 1877 he went to your town from Derby, that he lodged at an eating-house kept by a man who was in the habit of visiting the port for the purpose of soliciting sailors and others to lodge in his house, which was near the dock-walls, that detective-officers frequently went to the house to make inquiries, and that he remembers a boy being apprehended there who had absconded from Middlesbrough. In order to disguise himself he made himself a gutta-percha instrument which he wore on the left hand, and which gave him the appearance of a man with one arm. At the end of the arm, he states, he wore a hook, which, for the purposes of his meals, was replaced by a fork. He alleges that he committed two burglaries in Hull, whereof one was at a public-house on the Spring Bank, where he stole a quantity of cigars and some cash.—I have the honour to be, etc.,

C. E. H. VINCENT, Director.

One of Peace's most exciting burglaries of about this time was one that took place in the West End.

He had carefully spotted a likely house, and, night-time having duly arrived, he presented himself in the role of uninvited guest—his entrance being effected through the window.

Once inside, his boots were hastily slipped off. A hurried, yet stealthy ascent of a wide staircase leading to the top of the house, then he found himself at the door of what appeared to be a gentleman's sitting-room on the second floor.

Treading noiselessly on the pile carpet, he made an excursion over to the window according to his invariable habit, so as to ascertain what chanaces of escape it offered him in case of necessity. Pulling back the heavy curtain, he looked out. Bad! Very bad! The window looked right out on to the glass roof of a conservatory. No good seeking exit by that way. Well, never mind, he must return to work and chance all on the door. Still, he did not like.

Once more he made his way across the room to where stood the safe, which was the object of his quest. He was just in the act of kneeling down in front of it when his quick ears detected a slight sound behind him.

Quick as a shot he sprang to his feet, only just in time! There, behind him, standing in the doorway and effectually preventing all chance of escape in that direction was the huge, towering form of a butler.

A glance sufficed to tell Peace that for once he had met more than his physical match. To attempt to come to grips with the servant could have but one result for him.

Instinctively he put his hand behind his back for his revolver. Lightning like the butler sprang upon him ere he could ge the weapon free. It was as much as he could do to wriggle away as his adversary came down upon him and to make a dart for the now undefended doorway.

No good The portal was guarded by another manservant who had come hastily on the scene. He was as tall and powerful as the first. What manner of house could this be, where they employed ex-pugilists and wrestlers as butlers and footmen?

The window! That meant a fall on to the glass conservatory roof, but the chance which before had not seemed worth considering, now had become the only one.

Smart then! No time must be lost. Up flew the sash and——— , Crash!

The men who had been giving chase but a moment before now stopped still, staring at one another as the ominous sound broke upon their startled ears.

"That's done for him!" said the first comer in tones half of regret, half of admiration. "A slippery customer he were, too, and almost a sin for to hand him over to the police, but he won't be wanting no police now." Yet the man was wrong. True, Peace had not escaped scatheless. The broken glass on to which he had fallen had so badly injured his foot that he was laid up from the effects of the found for months. But he got away, and he did it, too, before ever the servants who had come so near to capturing him thought of looking to make sure whether he was dead or alive.

How he managed to make good his escape in his terribly wounded condition, leaving no tell-tale tracks of blood behind him, is perhaps in its way as wonderful as anything else in the man's marvellous history.

STANDING IN THE DOORWAY WAS THE HUGE TOWERING FORM OF THE BUTLER

However, he managed it. That much we do know.

On another occasion during Peace's sojourn in the metropolis he happened to attract the attention of police while "loitering about for an unlawful purpose" in the neighborhood of Westbourne Park.

Without knowing the man's identity, the smart young detective officer who had seen him hanaging around a certain block of houses during the day time formed the shrewd conclusion that the burglar—as he felt sure the man to be—would revisit the same black at night under still more compromising circumstances.

Accordingly he reported the matter at the local police-station, with the result that the following trap was laid for Peace on his return:—

After the inhabitants of the house in question had retired for the night a long piece of black thread was tied to the railings and right round the block, so that anyone attempting to enter or leave must perforce break it.

Police were posted at intervals to watch the thread and raise the alarm the moment they saw it give.

Presently it broke. The alarm was given, and the constables closed in on the instant. So smartly had the manoeuvre been effected it seemed impossible for the bird to escape.

But, smart as they were, they were not as quick as Peace. All the reward they got for their cuteness was a momentary vision of their man springing over a high fence like a panther, ere he vanished as he had come.

Truly Peace had the agility of a wild animal.

A visit of his to Southampton is also famous, because it disclosed a side of Peace's character which is so full of human interest that one cannot help thinking the man was a burglar as much from the love of adventure as from the desire for gain.

He "Called" at the office of a wealthy shipowner who lived in the neighbourhood of Above Bar. The offices were situated in a quiet portion of the town, and Peace had no difficulty in reaching the goal of his expedition—the safe.

But the job proved rather tougher than he anticipated. Expert safe-breaker as he was, it looked for the moment as if the night's work would be wasted, when he bethought himself of a plan which was so simple that it could only have occurred to the determined man he undoubtedly was.

He hunted about the office till he discovered the shipowner's address. Having found it, he sought out the house and proceeded to search for the keys of the safe.

All the while the family were asleep upstairs.

High and low he hunted, but without success. The keys, he thought, must be in one room, and in one room only—that occupied by the gentleman on whom he was so thoughtfully "calling."

Peace never stopped to think twice. He took off his boots, opened the bedroom door, crept around the bed, and found the sleeper's trousers hanging from the bedpost. In another moment, with the keys in his hand, he was running back to the office.

But, alas, after all his trouble the safe contained only a few pounds. Disgusted beyond all measure he annexed a big bundle of papers, so that his visit, though a financial failure, should give the greatest possible trouble.

Fifteen minutes afterwards he was in the train, examining at leisure the stolen documents.

What was his surprise to discover amongst them his "host's" will.

Peace always said that after reading the document through he came to the conclusion that the property it referred to had been so fairly distributed that the least he could do would be to return the will to its owner—an act of grace which he performed without delay.

It is believed that this was not the only occasion on which he sent back to its owners property which he considered had either a purely sentimental value or no value at all.

Out of the proceeds of the Southampton burglary he presented Mrs. Ward and Sue Thompson with five pounds each. To Willie he gave half a sovereign.

During the time he was living at Peckham he committed the following burglaries amongst others:—

In Richmond Road, Honor Oak: Thirty pounds' worth of goods.
Langham Road, Streatham: Silk dress and £30 in plate.
At Kidbrook Terrace, Blackheath: Jewellery.
At Herne Hill: Watches and plate.

These are only examples of the kind of work in which he was engaged. He committed scores of other burglaries, large and small.

Before he "did a job" he was always as careful as ever to spy out the land. He took long drives with the pony and trap.

As an illustration of the use to which the trap was put the following extraordinary story is told.

Peace ever had his eye on the large houses that were scattered around London. One of the most attractive of them, from his point of view, was the mansion at Chislehurst, then occupied by the Empress Eugenie and Prince Louis Napoleon.

One day the familiar trap turned up in the neighbourhood, and Peace might have been seen taking a quiet stroll. He walked round and round the mansion mentally noting all sorts of useful details. But the outside was not the inside, of which he had to know something if any "business" was to be done.

His wits came to the rescue, as usual, for he played the following trick upon the unsuspecting agent.

Knowing that the Empress was away, he wrote, asking permission to inspect the house with his "architect," as he "wished to build himself a large villa in the same style."

The permission was evidently given, for after Peace's arrest a plan of the house was found in Evelina Road. Upon it was noted every detail that would be of assistance to a gentleman of Peace's profession, but happily he never had an opportunity of testing its accuracy.

Yet Peace was not always waging war upon society.

He was a creature of so many contradictions that, astounded as one may be on hearing it, one must believe when one learns that he was interested in several patents. At all events, there is the following record in the "Patent Gazette":—

2635. *Henry Forsey Brion, 22, Philip Road, Peckham Rye, London, S. E., and John Thompson, 5, East Terrace, Evelina Road, Peckham Rye, London, S. E., for an invention for raising sunken vessels by the displacement of water within the vessels by air or gases.*

Peace and Brion were friends for many months.

They made each other's acquaintance under peculiar circumstances. A child was run over near Peace's house one day, and Mr. Brion called on his neighbour, "Mr. Thompson," to ask if he had heard how the little one was getting on.

"One thing led to another," as they say, and Mr. Brion was soon talking about his inventions. It was not long before they discovered that they had much in common, and Brion became a regular visitor at the house.

Let us do Peace the justice of saying that apart from any mutual benefit that might accrue through the two helping in the working out of each other's patents, the friendship appears to have been quite disinterested on both sides.

Speaking of this phase of his career, Mrs. Thompson once said that Charles Peace's patent for raising sunken vessels was regarded in many quarters as a great success. She remembered Peace making a model ship eight feet long which, by his compressed air scheme, could be sunk and raised three times in eight minutes.

He was present, she said, at two experiments with it which took place near Westminster and London bridges.

There is some ground for believing that Peace regarded the invention seriously, for in the year 1879 Mr. Roger Moore, the hon. secretary of the Plimsoll Life at Sea Association, stated that he was staying with Mr. Plimsoll in the early part of '78 when two persons— presumably Peace and Brion—called and said they wished to submit a scheme for raising the "Vanguard" and the "Captain."

As they were strangers, Mr. Plimsoll declined to receive them, but later in the day they saw him at the House of Commons, and wished him to introduce them to the First Lord of the Admiralty. Mr. Plimsoll declined to have anything to do with them.

THE LIFE STORY OF CHARLES PEACE

The incident is certainly characteristic of the man. Imagine it: the Banner Cross murderer coolly talking to an M. P. in the House and a reward of a hundred pounds out for his capture. Only Peace would have done that.

Towards the end of Peace's life we find this association of Peace and Brion over their inventions brought forward once more in the form of a deed of gift drawn up in Armley gaol, where the former was lying under sentence of death.

To Mr. Henry F. Brion, 22, Philip Road, Peckham Rye.
H. M. Prison, Leeds, February 20th, 1879.

I, Charles Peace, freely and without cost, herewith of my own accord, give to Mr. Henry Brion my inventions as follows:—
  1. *Invention for supplying members of fire-brigades and others with pure air when buildings are on fire.*
  2. *Improved brush for washing railway-carriages, etc.*
  3. *Hydraulic tank for supply of water.*

(Signed) CHARLES PEACE.

WITNESSES: *Oswald Cookson, M. A., Chaplain H. M. Prison, Leeds; G. G. Graves.*

If these inventions were really the property of Peace he must be given credit for an extraordinary brain. Once again the student of the man's career is forced to the admission that but for an unfortunate flaw in his construction Peace might have been not only a useful member of society, but an ornament. It seems incredible that Peace should have thought of the smoke-helmet which has been such a boon to firemen and miners. One never knows what to believe about the man.

One more incident relative to Peace's home-life. It is short in the extreme, but so grimly prophetic that it cannot well be omitted. It is given in Sue Thompson's own words.

"Once we went to Madame Tussaud's Exhibition. He (Peace) said he wanted to look for diamonds on the wax figures.

"He asked me to go into the Chamber of Horrors with him, but I refused.

"'Perhaps,' said I, 'I may see your model there yet.'

"He was very angry with me for saying that. As I would not accompany him he took Mrs. Ward."

Within a year of this incident the following advertisement appeared in the London papers:—

MADAME TUSSAUD'S.

Portrait model representing Peace, the Banner Cross murderer, disguised as Mr. Thompson, of Blackheath, and also as he appeared in convict-dress on his trial, taken from life, added to the Chamber of Horrors.

The Day of Retribution was indeed at hand.

The voice of a prophet had spoken through the mouth of the treacherous Sue Thompson.

CHAPTER XIII.
A Few More Burglaries.

Perhaps of all the burglaries committed by Peace that which yielded him the greatest monetary return was one committed at Melton Mowbray.

It took place at the family seat of a well-known nobleman. That Peace should ever have attempted it at all is only another instance of the man's colossal daring.

The house—or should we say castle?—stood in the centre of a fine estate not far from the town. From the housebreaker's point of view, however, the job was rendered extremely difficult by the fact that the drive where it approached the entrance was flanked by nothing more than dwarfed shrubs. These would afford the scantiest cover for prowlers to lurk beneath.

On the other hand, anyone could boldly pass the porter's lodge even after dark by saying he had business with the nobleman owning the estate.

Peace decided on the latter course.

Up the drive he sauntered. Soon, very soon, thanks to the bareness of the landscape, he came within sight of the windows.

A quick glance and he had located that belonging to the strong room. He continued his way right up to the great oaken door, and placed his hand upon the bell pull. He even went so far as to give it the slightest jerk, so that if he had been seen approaching the servants would answer it in the ordinary way, merely thinking he had failed to pull hard enough to make the bell ring through unfamiliarity with the mechanism.

If they came he had his story ready. Then he would have to go away like an honest man, leaving the burglary till another night.

A minute went by, but no servant appeared. Good! That meant the coast was clear. He had not been seen.

A quick turn round the angle of the porch, a clutch at a low hanging branch of creeper, and he was swinging up the wall with the agility of a wild cat.

Nearer and nearer he came to the strong room window. At last he was as near to it as the creeper would take him.

An agile spring and he had hold of the iron grid that protected the casement on the outside. Then a quarter of an hour's hard unceasing toil with an oiled file, and two of the bars were moved sufficiently far out of position to admit of the burglar's body passing through the aperture.

Now to settle the window-pane. In these days of improved forms of protection against burglary, Peace would have found it a very difficult task to break into a strong room. In the first place, it is usual to build them now without windows at all. But in the seventies the protection given by good stout iron bars was commonly thought to be enough for all practical purposes, even where, as in this case, the worth of the valuables stored within was very considerable.

A few cuts with a good diamond, a smart tap with the open palm, after shrouding the pane in brown paper rendered sticky with treacle, so as to prevent broken bits clattering down and making a noise, and the thing was done.

Inside, the burglar cautiously opened the shutter of his dark lantern and took stock of the place.

He was in what appeared to be a passage, opening out of which were two doors. These he rightly guessed to belong to the two strong rooms, in the one of which—that nearest to the inner door of the passage—the butler stored the gold and silver plate, while the door nearest himself would open on to the room where lay the nobleman's private heirlooms, jewellery mostly, and valuables worth thousands of pounds at the very least.

This second, then, was the door of which Peace had come in search. So well did he carry out his intentions that within an hour afterwards he had gained the window-sill once more and was proceeding to lower himself over it, his coat pockets bulging with gold and precious stones worth more than four thousand pounds.

A haul that! No wonder the success of it made Peace for once in his life a trifle reckless. He forgot to look beneath him ere he lowered his legs over the sill.

It had been his intention to let himself down in this way as far as possible, holding on to the sill by his hands in the hope of finding a foothold somewhere in the wall below by which he could continue his descent.

Failing that, there would be nothing for it but to let go bodily and drop in the wild hope that a frantic clutch at the creeper on the way down would pull him up in time.

The latter was a wild alternative. Still, just then Peace was in no mood to care. He had done almost as risky things in his time. Besides, when a man has the equivalent of over four thousand pounds in his pocket as the result of a single successful haul, he is not in the mood to dwell on difficulties over much.

So Peace let down his legs. Forward and backward he drew them to find a chink wherein his feet might come to rest; but no chink did he find.

Then he moved one foot out a little bit to ease it, as it was getting stiff.

Curious. Almost immediately it came to rest on a support that gave slightly under him as he placed his weight on it, but otherwise it seemed firm enough.

He tried the effect of adding the weight of his other foot to this odd and unexplained support. Only a trifle more give. Whatever it was it showed no serious signs of breaking. But what was it?

For the first time he looked beneath him.

It was a ladder.

At the same moment his ears caught the sound of hoarse shouting coming up from the grounds below.

Caught! Caught like a rat in a trap, and just when he thought he had brought off the most successful robbery of his life. What should he do?

In an instant his mind was made up.

Bending himself down till his hands grasped the top rung of the ladder, he swung from bar to bar with the almost incredible rapidity of a monkey swinging rom perch to perch.

Whatever else happened now, one thing he was determined on: either he would get away with his booty or be torn to pieces in the attempt. And woe to the man who tried to stop him.

It was not long before Peace had the opportunity of putting this precept into action.

Half-way down the ladder he bumped against the body of a gardener who was ascending in the hope of effecting his capture.

Out shot the burglar's fist with the force of a ram-rod, even while with the other hand he clung for dear life to the ladder, and over-pitched the gardener with a hollow groan.

There came the sound of a heavy body crashing on the gravel of the drive below followed by mingled screams and cries of execration from those assembled round about, but Peace was not troubling him self about anyone else.

Now or never was his chance to effect his escape. Only a few more rungs now and he would be within leaping distance of the ground. Then for——

But his thoughts were never completed. At that moment a rush was made for the foot of the ladder.

A wild heave, and Peace felt himself shaken from it, and hurtling through the air as the unfortunate gardener had done before him. Wild with rage, the other servants had deliberately thrown the ladder down with its human burden still upon it.

Crack! The air was filled with splintered wood as rungs and sides split and scattered round about. In the midst of the havoc they had created, the servants put their hands to their faces and rushed wildly away to avoid the falling debris.

Of them all only two remained alert enough to pounce on the little man who had been the cause of all the commotion, and who just then dropped to the earth, only to bound up again with the lightness of a panther and spring for the open.

For the two Peace was more than a match. Smack, smack! One,

OUT SHOT THE BURGLAR'S FIST. Page 70

two! and those who had tried to stop him bit the dust, leaving a clear field for his escape.

Off he bounded quick as a rocket. No following a human fiend who flew over ground like that.

In the hurry of the moment the bloodhounds had been forgotten. Only now were they thought of, when it was really too late.

A wild dash round to the stables where were their kennels. They were free and baying now with all the fury of the chase as they raced madly out on to the lawn.

A minute's delay in putting them on the scent. Ah! they were off at last. Away they went.

But Charles Peace had too good a start.

The great dogs followed him seemingly for miles, but in the early hours of the morning the servants returned to the castle to inform the nobleman that the thief had got safely away with the booty.

And Charles Peace? What did he think of it all?

It is said that in after days he was wont to recall that particular burglary as one of the most treasured in his memory.

"Not because it happened to be one where I made perhaps as big a haul as ever I did," he would explain, "but because, when I saw I'd bungled over the ladder business, I set myself to get away with the swag or give up the trade for good and all; and I got away."

How much better for him if he had not got away.

Yet if the above incident shows forth something of the luck that usually attended the murderer's burglarious exploits, it absolutely pales into insignificance before the mixture of good fortune and sheer audacity that aided Peace on the occasion of his theft of a lady's valuable jewellery from a railway train.

The jewels themselves were contained in a jewel-case which had been left on the seat in a first-class compartment while the owner, a wealthy society woman, went to the refreshment-room of the station where the train was at rest to obtain some lunch.

In those days corridor trains and luncheon cars were unknown, in England at any rate. The lady in question had left her maid to keep guard over the valuables, and she in her turn had left her trust for the minute to speak to a friend on the platform.

That minute was more than enough for Peace. Quick as lightning he saw his chance, and, boarding the train, snatched up the jewel-case and concealed it under his frock-coat.

A quick walk towards the exit. There an unpleasant surprise awaited him. Standing right in the doorway was a police detective whom he recognised at once, and who moreover, he felt equally sure, would very soon recognise him unless he shifted, and that quickly.

What should he do?

He could not leave the station. He could not replace the jewels now even if he wanted to, for already their disappearance had been discovered. In a moment the station would be alive with people

THE LIFE STORY OF CHARLES PEACE

searching for the probable thief, and then the detective would be the first to see him and arrest him on suspicion.

Suddenly a bright idea occurred to him. In ten minutes or less the train would have started. If he could only lie low till then all might yet be well—for him. But where? What would afford him a hiding-place?

A quick glance round about. The platform was hopeless, likewise the waiting and refreshment rooms. Ah!

For at that moment a chance had presented itself to him. The top of the railway carriage!

That was the one alternative to exposure and prison. But it must be taken at once if at all.

For the moment no one was within sight of the end buffers of the train.

A run. A leap. A scramble. It was done.

The officials and police might search the station through and through now for the jewels and the jewel thief without result—unless they happened to look on the roof of the foremost of the railway carriages.

For that was where Charles Peace was lying at full length, unsuspected by all, while right beneath him, divided only by a thin roof, busy railway officials were taking notes of the robbery.

At last it was done. The lady had been calmed as much as possible by the promise of the speedy return by the police of her pet playthings. The careless maid had been duly reduced to hysterics.

The engine puffed. The train moved. It was going now, faster, faster, gaining speed with every second.

And there, clinging for dear life to the roof boards and ventilators of the front carriage was Peace, with the jewel-case safe in one of the capacious pockets of his coat.

Five minutes went by and the train did not slacken speed. Ten minutes, and still no sign of stopping. By now the criminal's arms were beginning to ache painfully. How much longer would he be able to hold on?

Look! What was this the train was coming to? Could it be a tunnel? Every second now the banks on either side of the line were becoming higher and higher.

Cautiously Peace raised his head as much as he dared and looked.

Yes, it was a tunnel. What would happen to the fugitive in its murky depths, amidst the smother of steam and smoke, to say nothing of flying sparks?

Even as the thought struck him, the engine shrieked and plunged into the abyss of blackness. Into the tunnel swept the engine. As it whirled into the blackness Peace almost gave himself up for lost.

What if the top of the tunnel should prove so low as to sweep him from the roof? In imagination he could feel already the terrible crash with which his head would come into contact with the hard stone of the roof arch. And then——

The carriage had swung into the yawning tunnel mouth. It was travelling now like mad into the inky void beyond.

Peace was still clutching the ventilators and thus managing somehow to keep his place, for all that the rails inside the tunnel were less well-laid than those in the open, so that the train oscillated more than ever as it pursued its headlong course.

Phew! How the smoke of the engine's funnel swept back upon him and suffocated him. Would the train never slow down? Peace tried to cough out the fumes that filled his lungs, but the draft only forced them further and further down.

It was torture—nothing less. If only he had known what he was in for when he stole the jewel-case! How glad would he not have been to have left it safely on the seat of the compartment underneath where he was now hiding.

A second shriek from the steam whistle, positively deafening as it echoed forth in the confined space, and like a flash the train emerged from the tunnel as it had entered.

Once again all around was green, open country. Brilliant sunlight poured down on the prostrate man who but a moment since had been engulfed in blackness as of night. The smother of fumes and coal dust that had been slowly choking him to death tailed off into a harmless grey band of steamy vapour.

Once again the Master Criminal tried to get rid of the poisonous gases that had been fast reducing him to insensibility. This time he succeeded more or less.

Then, best of all, the train began to slow down. A quick glance over the carriage side revealed the fact that a station was being reached. It was one of those wayside junctions far away from the nearest village or hamlet and presided over by a single sleepy-eyed porter who was taking duty while his official superior, the station-master, regaled himself with a hot lunch in the station-house.

What could be better for Peace's plans? Presently the train would stop, but just before it did so he would have slipped off the rear buffer and have gained the main road that led up to the station entrance.

A minute or so and the train did stop. In those days railway travelling was a far more laboured affair than now. It might have been almost five minutes before the station-master appeared at the door of the station-house to signal "all right" before the restarting.

As he did so a queer-looking individual was seen to emerge from the booking-office.

He was a little man with a very big mouth, dressed in a frockcoat that bulged slightly at one side.

In one hand he clutched his hat, in the other the first-class ticket which he had just obtained, while his general air of breathlessness and disarray proclaimed the fact that he had had a tough run for it to catch his train at all.

Straight as a die he ran to the door of the carriage in which sat the lady still mourning the loss of her valuables, threw it open, and sat down opposite to her.

The train is on the move again. At first the theft of her jewels so absorbs the lady's mind she can hardly spare a thought for the newcomer. Presently, however, she is forced to notice him. He is speaking to her.

"Excuse me, madam, I fear you are somewhat fatigued with your journey. Perhaps the compartment is a trifle hot for you. May I suggest that if you had the window open——"

It is the leading note for which, though she does not herself suspect it, the lady has been waiting. It gives her the chance of unburdening herself to a sympathetic listener, a chance which she is not slow to avail herself of.

And Charles Peace is remarkably sympathetic. What is more, he is wonderfully practical, too. No sooner has he heard of the robbery of the jewel-case than he offers a whole series of most valuable suggestions as to how best the thief may be brought to book.

Needless to say, Peace got clear away after this sequence of experiences, and no one would have known a word about his true connection with them had he not chosen to leave behind him the record from which the facts have been got together.

CHAPTER XIV.

Peace the Jester.

That Peace was intensely human, and, withal, possessed of an immense fund of dry humour there is proof in abundance.

Sometimes even he proved the truth of the old saying that we are none of us too clever to be taken in by falling a victim to the attentions of a brother crook!

One story of him in particular brings into prominence all three traits in his character, and also shows how by the introduction of his ever-ready fund of impudence he managed to come out top after all.

It is the story of Peace on the racecourse.

On that occasion finding himself jammed in a crowd he took advantage of his opportunity to insert his hand into the coat pocket of a prosperous-looking gentleman standing next to him arrayed in frock-coat and top hat.

As a reward of agiiity he withdrew it clasping an object that glittered strangely as it momentarily caught the light.

Soon Peace was out of the crowd and away in a quiet corner of the course surveying his prize in quietude. It turned out to be a massive gold curb watchchain, each link being stamped with the crown and numerals constituting the Government hall-mark for eighteen carat quality.

Clearly the chain was a valuable one. Peace looked at it once and mentally thanked his luck as he remembered the queer chance by which he had got hold of it. He looked at it a second time. This time his brows suddenly contracted.

Still a little more hesitation while link by link was passed through the sinewy fingers of the prince of burglars. His mind was made up.

As he came to the decision, Charles Peace laughed a short, almost silent, laugh. Then he strolled back to the more frequented part of the course. Presently his eye lit upon the man he wanted—a bookie of the extra slippery fraternity.

Strolling up to him with the air of a man who has lost heavily and become consequently reckless, he held out the chain for his inspection.

"Here," he said, "I've put all I had on losers, and now I haven't got so much as a bob left to try my luck again. What'll you give me for this chain? It's a real good 'un as you can see, stamped on every link. I only want a few pounds just to see if my luck turns, and the chain's worth a tenner to anyone at the very least."

With a quick glance at the reckless man before him, the bookie took the chain, glanced at it, and handed Peace three sovereigns. The weight of the chain and the hall-marking on the links told him it was good for more than double that amount in pledge. So he parted with the three pounds readily enough, little dreaming he was really getting the worst of the bargain.

All the same, he must have been somewhat surprised when, instead of stopping to put the money on more losers, Peace muttered something unintelligible and edged behind a clump of loiterers and out of sight.

As a matter of fact, the explanation of it all was simple enough. The chain was what is known to the thieving world as a "duffman," or worthless imitation, in which the hall-mark is forged. Peace, without knowing it, had picked the pocket of a professional "racecourse swindler."

A "duffman" chain made of brass and merely gilded over the surface will cost the one in the know a few shillings, while simulating a value of many pounds. But there is a little tell-tale something about it that may generally be seen by the excessively sharp-eyed and which Peace certainly saw on this occasion.

The "duffman" nearly always has the "hall-mark" imperfectly stamped.

Usually it is a part of the crown that is either missing, or else not of the same shape as that on the genuine article. Few people except jewellers know to each little twist and turn exactly what a hall-mark should be like, and the spurious watchchain is made for the deception of the general public, and more especially that section

THE LIFE STORY OF CHARLES PEACE

of it which is to be found on racing nights in public-house bars in a more or less advanced state of intoxication. Hence the carelessness on the part of the manufacturer.

What the bookie said when he found out how he had been done history does not record.

Here is another true story of Charles Peace when residing at Evelina Road, Peckham. Like the last, it shows up the man as a jester of no mean order.

One day he went into a chemist's shop smoking a cigar. It was not the kind of cigar that folk usually smoked in Peckham, and the chemist detected it at once.

"Nice cigar, that, Mr. Thompson," he said, sniffing delicately at the fragrant fumes.

"Yes," said Peace, with a strange twinkle in his eye.

"Where did you get it from?"

"Oh, I stole it," said the old fellow quietly.

The shopkeeper laughed at the very thought of it.

"Stolen, indeed! Well, I wish you'd steal a few for me."

"Certainly," replied Peace; "you shall have some the very next time I come into the shop."

Sure enough a week or two afterwards Peace looked in again. In his hand was a box of choice cigars, which he threw on to the counter with a careless "There you are! I've stolen those for you!"

Peace afterwards related this incident to the late Major Arthur Griffiths, then assistant governor of Armley Gaol—his last "residence"—as an illustration of his pet theory—the bolder your tactics the greater your security.

But as capping all that has gone before, we cannot forbear to touch on a story told of him which shows him up in the light of a man of as great humour as he undoubtedly possessed resource.

One day when returning by train to Peckham after a visit of inspection to a likely crib, he found himself in a compartment with a little red-haired fellow. This little man by some freak of chance took him for a detective and accordingly engaged him in conversation with a view to pumping him of the official theory regarding the latest of the Peckham burglaries.

At first Peace, who was not in loquacious mood, tried to put his travelling companion off with short answers. No use. The red-haired man would have none of it. He stuck to the pumping process, and in due time turned out to be a small suburban tradesman.

At last Peace conceived a quaint idea.

"Look here," he said, "what's the use of expecting us detectives to know exactly how every robbery on the face of the earth is accomplished? There must be some limit to our powers you know. Besides, you've no idea of the 'cuteness criminals show in going about their business. Some of them could beat me hollow in that direction.

and, as a detective, I know a thing or two myself. For instance, I'd guarantee to break into your shop and open the safe in your office without your knowing anything about it, although I'd previously told you the exact night the entrance was going to take place."

"Nonsense; it's impossible! You couldn't do it." The alarmed tradesman's hair began to show distinct signs of standing on end.

"Couldn't I?" said Peace, and he laughed good-humouredly. "You try me, that's all. Tell me what night I shall break into your place and what I shall take out from the safe to show you I've actually kept my word. Then I only require your word to go to bed in the ordinary way and not to stir from your room unless you hear a sound. If you do, then come down and catch me redhanded, and I'll pay you five pounds for your 'cuteness. How's that?"

The red-haired man mopped his forehead excitedly. He was beginning by now to feel heartily sorry he had forced the detective into conversation. Those official gentlemen did so take the bull by the horns. All the same it was a fine opportunity of testing the strength of the safe and his own sharpness of hearing also, to say nothing of the fiver he would make if he caught the other at his self-imposed task.

"Yes, I agree. I'll lock up this handkerchief as a test."

Very well. Peace took the whole arrangement as coolly as though it had been an invitation to call in the evening for a friendly smoke. He took down the tradesman's address on his cuff, and soon the train drew in at the station where he was to alight.

"I'll make my call tonight," were his last words as he shook hands with his new-found acquaintance.

He did make his call that night. As might be expected, entrance to the shop was simple child's play to one of his experience. Nor was the safe such a tough job either. Soon he had it open. The handkerchief was duly withdrawn from the interior; and then a strange thing happened.

He kicked against the safe in the act of shutting it again. The sound echoed through the house. Almost immediately a door above opened, and there came the sound of feet pattering down the stairs.

The red-haired man was arrayed in nightshirt and trousers. In one hand he grasped a candlestick, in the other a poker. His face was the colour of candle grease, while his hands shook so with fright at the thought that it might be a real burglar after all that they set both poker and candlestick dancing before Peace's eyes like marionettes.

As soon as the little fellow saw it was only his friend of the afternoon returned, he gave forth a hollow cry of thankfulness and collapsed on to the nearest easy-chair.

"Oh, lor!" he gasped, "what a turn you have given me. And—and—you've done it, too. Who'd have thought it?"

For Peace was holding up the handkerchief for his inspection.

Presently, however, the tradesman regained his equanimity. He asked for a glass of whisky and pointed to the cupboard where it was kept. In the cupboard were two glasses. That was increasingly fortunate. By the time ten minutes had been spent in friendly explanations of how it was done, the two were in the best of spirits again.

At last, though without hurry, the "detective" took his leave, not before paying up his fiver like a man.

Only when examining the safe next morning did our red-haired friend discover that, besides the handkerchief, loose cash in gold and notes had been removed from it to the tune of nearly a hundred and fifty pounds. Then he, too, began to realize how extremely 'cute some criminals are.

A careful examination of the five-pound note with which the "detective" had paid his lost wager disclosed the fact that it was actually a part of the "haul" resulting from the robbery of the safe five minutes before.

Surely if Peace has not already made good his title of "Prince of Jesters" of the criminal fraternity, this account must go far towards conferring it on him.

CHAPTER XV.

Peace Meets an Imitator.

Like all great men, be they statesmen or criminals, Peace had his imitators.

How many he had it is impossible to say.

But head and shoulders above all the rest stands the figure of one imitator in particular.

This man must have been really something far above the ordinary as criminals go.

Peace's robberies numbered hundreds, and towards the end of his career he invariably got off without detection. The robberies of his imitator numbered at least two score from first to last, and he too, so far as is known, was never captured.

He was a first-rate understudy to a leading actor—almost on a level with his superior in everything except originality.

Who was this imitator?

No one knows. He was never caught, or, if he was, was never identified as the author of what were known as the later Blackheath robberies.

The only thing which showed the police the robberies in question were the work of an imitator at all and not of Peace himself was the fact that a dozen or more of them all planned and carried out on Peace's system were perpetrated after the master mind was safely enclosed in prison walls.

Here is a typical newspaper paragraph taken from the "Daily

Telegraph" of January 20th, 1879, which we give as a case in point.

"Another burglar, supposed to be an imitator of Charles Peace, has turned up at Blackheath. Early yesterday morning he made an attempt to enter the house of Mr. Marsh, which is situated in an isolated spot between the villages of Blackheath and Old Charlton. Since the recent burglaries in this locality the residents have provided themselves with firearms, and in this case Mr. Marsh had recourse to his revolver. He fired three times at the burglar, who escaped. The firing attracted the attention of the police, who scoured the neighbourhood for the offender, but without success."

There is the record of one of over two score of burglaries and attempted burglaries committed by this imitator of the master criminal.

Who and what sort of man was he?

For the answer we must go to Charles Peace himself.

Peace met him.

The occasion was in this wise.

Peace was out on burglary bent. The house he had spotted for the occasion belonged to a wealthy Blackheath resident, the date of the robbery scarcely a month previous to his arrest by Police-constable Robinson.

Once again we follow the central figure of our story as he creeps up to a low side entrance.

A flash from the dark lantern, come and gone again in a moment. It is sufficient. Peace has whipped a skeleton key from among his set and is inserting it in the lock.

Click! The bolt shoots back. How often have we followed him on similar expeditions. But this time a startling surprise is in store.

Inside the mansion Peace felt his way from the servants' quarters along the pitchy dark passages to the part occupied by the householder and his family.

On either hand old oak panelling, the walls hung with rare pictures and trophies of the chase elaborately mounted in silver. No wonder Peace, as he neared the foot of the main staircase, paused with watering mouth at the sight of it all.

And then, as he turned his gaze almost straight ahead, the light of the dark lantern swept round in a quarter circle till it rested on the glass of a huge full-length mirror fronting the staircase.

In the dim radiance the sheen of the glass was unobservable.

Peace looked. At the same moment there came a hurried click from the staircase by the side of which he was standing.

Ah! What was that?

He was looking at something, the light of a second dark lantern shining on him from out of the mirror.

But it was not that which caused his momentary start of fear. It was something far different which the faint gleam of the answering light revealed.

There, seemingly standing before him, and in the same half-

THE LIFE STORY OF CHARLES PEACE

crouching attitude was—himself. Short, diminutive of stature, bulging forehead, slit-like mouth—there was no mistaking the tell-tale features.

A moment to pull his shattered nerves together, and he took a determined step forward.

As he moved the figure moved also, though in a slightly different way. Clearly this was no ordinary looking-glass reflection. What was it?

For perhaps another ten seconds Charles Peace stood staring at the reflection in the mirror, while great drops of perspiration came out on his forehead.

He was no chicken heart, far from it, but this dim and shadowy form that floated in front of him, and which was and yet was not him, what could it be?

One moment he was gazing at it aghast.

The next the truth, or something of the truth, burst in upon him.

It was a mirror that he stood in front of, a great, full-length looking-glass. Yes, but even then was it only his reflection that he saw?

A slight alteration of the direction of the beam of light from his own bull's-eye lantern. As he made it he could see a second still more vague and undefined form spring up in the mirror and gaze at him with fixed horror-struck eyes.

A quick movement of the feet by way of experiment. It was imitated on the instant by this second shadow. That, then, was his true reflection. But the other one which remained motionless, gazing at him with a look of haunted fascination that utterly eclipsed his own, once more, what was it, or who was he?

And then from the stairs came a sharp, indrawn hiss of breath. The reflection shuddered, started, and assumed an erect posture. Convulsively it opened its lips to speak, but no sound came from them.

Once again the same convulsive and fruitless attempt, then the words:

"Charles Peace!"

With the snarl of a panther the master criminal bounded up the great staircase towards the one who had spoken. All his fears were gone now, submerged in the realisation of deadly peril that came from the knowledge he had been recognised.

"Who are you?" he hissed. "Quick, or I fire. How is it you recognise me when all the police of London have failed?"

And then, even as he covered that other one cowering now before him on the stairs, his arm shook and dropped to his side through sheer astonishment.

He had been astounded when he caught sight of what he believed to be his double in the looking-glass, and here it stood before him in flesh and blood, and consequently ten times more astounding than ever.

It was a man the very image of Peace himself, so much so that as he craned his head forward the better to see him in the light of the dark lantern Peace found it hard to believe it was other than his own self he was looking at.

For a moment the similarity was complete. Then Peace got control of himself, and, reaching forth his hand, with a lightning-like movement caught at his imitator's hair.

In vain the fellow tried to ward off the attack. There was a scuffle, a few sweeping motions of the arms, and the make-up was torn off.

With a low, sarcastic laugh, Charles Peace threw the wig, false eyebrows, and the rest of the paraphernalia he had wrenched off from the impostor on to the carpet.

"Stand up!" he commanded peremptorily.

Shaking with fright, the imitator stood erect, revealing himself as a man nearly four inches Peace's superior in height.

Peace surveyed him as a schoolmaster might survey a naughty schoolboy, and grunted:

"Well, what's the game? Why did you do it?"

What followed after that it is not possible to give in detail. It is known the man explained as well as he could how his reading of the marvellous exploits of Peace had fired him with ardour to do likewise. To the confession the arch-criminal listened with ill-concealed contempt.

At the conclusion of it he actually proceeded to ensconce himself in a comfortable position on the stairs, insisting that his new acquaintance should do likewise, and totally unmindful of the danger the two ran of being disturbed by the householder in the middle of the conversation which ensued.

And it was a conversation, too. Peace told his imitator what he thought of such tomfoolery in no measured terms, ending by marching him out of the kitchen entrance to the side door of the house.

This happening to be locked, and the key removed from the inside, Peace picked the lock with one hand, while firmly holding on to his double with the other. Finally, when the portal was open he kicked the man outside, and threw his make-up after him.

Unlike the present-day actor, Peace evidently was no believer in hero-worship.

CHAPTER XVI

The Arrest by P. C. Robinson.

One night Mr. Thompson did not come home as usual.
He did not come home the next night——
Nor the next——
Nor at all.
Of course not. He had "gone abroad."
Mrs. Thompson said so.

THE LIFE STORY OF CHARLES PEACE

* * * * * *

Where had he gone to?

"*At Greenwich Police-court yesterday,*" *said the London* Daily Chronicle *on October 11th,* 1878, "*a man about fifty years of age, half-caste, who refused his name and address, was charged with burglariously entering Gifford House, St. John's Park, Blackheath, and stealing silver and plated and other articles, and also with discharging five chambers of shot of a six-chambered revolver and wounding Police-constable Robinson,* 202 R, *by shooting him through the right arm.*

The prisoner was a curious-looking individual. His head and face were so bandaged up that it was impossible to see much of his features; but enough was to be seen to show that he was extremely ugly. He had a long, coarse slit of a mouth, huge nostrils that looked like the snout of a wild animal, ferrety eyes, and tremendously-developed forehead that seemed to go up to the crown of his head.

The evidence was to the effect that at two o'clock in the morning Robinson called the attention of Constable Girling to a light in the back dining-room of Gifford House, the residence of Mr. J. A. Barnass. The two constables thereupon stationed themselves on top of the garden wall, where they sat whilst the light moved all about the house from the top to the bottom.

When they had been sitting on the wall for three-quarters of an hour Sergeant Brown came up. They reported what they had seen, whereupon the sergeant ordered them to remain where they were whilst he went round to the front door and rang the bell.

At the sound of the bell the light was suddenly extinguished.

Robinson at once jumped into the garden and Girling into the avenue, so that they could cut off the escape of the supposed burglar.

No sooner was he in the garden than Robinson saw a man dash from the dining-room window on to the lawn and run along the garden.

He at once gave chase, whereupon the man turned, presented a revolver, and said:

"Keep back, keep off, or I will shoot you!"

Disregarding the warning, Robinson rushed at the man, who met him with three shots, but inflicted no injury.

The constable made another rush.

This time the burglar took deliberate aim and fired again without inflicting any injury.

In a trice the constable was on to his man, whom he dealt a heavy blow in the face. But before he could raise his hand again the man shouted out:

"This time I'll settle you," and there was another report.

This shot took effect. It perforated the constable's great-coat, and went through his arm above the elbow.

The two closed. There was a struggle.

Down they went to the ground, and as they fell the constable wrenched the revolver from the man's waist, where it was secured by a strap, and dealt him a blow on the head with it.

By way of reply the prisoner put his left hand in his pocket, saying, "I'll give you something else."

Fortunately, at this moment the sergeant and the other constable came up. All three fell on to the burglar and "knocked him out."

For some minutes the three stood examining their captive by the light of a lantern. He looked like a half-caste.

Presently he revived, and lay where he fell, half dazed and grinning.

"You're a cowardly fellow," said Brown, holding up the revolver, "to come with a thing like this."

The burglar's mouth broadened out into a smile.

"May be," said Brown, "there will be some more of your people about?"

"Oh, no, there's not," replied the captive. "Take my word for it, I have no one with me."

"You're a nice one to ask us to take your word," said the constable. "We'll go and look for ourselves."

When Gifford House was searched it was found that the dining-room window had been forced by means of a jemmy and that a hole five inches square had been cut into the door near the lock, so that the burglar could put his hand through and unfasten the door.

A quantity of silver and plate had been put by ready for removal. A bank-book and some letters had also been taken.

Finally the half-caste in the garden had upon him a complete burglar's outfit, including a long jemmy in sections, which could be screwed together.

The prisoner refused to give the slightest information about himself. He was therefore remanded for a week, during which time a strange thing happened.

Question him as they would, the police could get nothing from him, till one day he asked to be allowed to drop a line to a friend of his. That was just what they wanted.

The permission readily granted, who should the mysterious half-caste write to but our old friend, Mr. Brion, of Peckham Rye.

In the letter, which was dated November 3rd, Peace begged his old friend to come and see him. He attributed his misfortune to drink, and spoke of the terrible position in which he was placed, of his loneliness, of his desire for friendship and help. He went on to beg Brion not to desert him in his hour of trouble. He professed the greatest shame and sorrow for his crime, and promised, if he were set free, to have nothing more to do with drink.

At first sight it would seem almost inconceivable that the man who had bested the finest detectives in England for so many months should have been so foolish as to fall into such a trap.

The fact remains that prisoners are particularly prone to make such false moves. Probably the reason is that in their former lives they have accustomed themselves to taking such reckless chances they have thereby lost the fine sensibility that enables the normal man to distinguish between a chance however desperate and a certainly fatal action.

Peace wanted the comfort of Brion's society, and in his desperate state was prepared to risk a lot for it. That there was more than mere risk attached to the sending of his letter he had lost the power of divining.

That letter gave the police sufficient information to enable them to charge the prisoner at the next hearing before the magistrate at Greenwich as John Ward.

They were wily enough on that occasion to say that nothing more was known about the prisoner.

They did know something, however.

They knew that a woman calling herself Thompson had been passing as his wife in Evelina Road.

Mr. Ward was very indignant when he heard that he was to be remanded for another week. He bitterly complained of such an injustice to a man who had never been in prison before.

He could not, of course, know that the police had run Mrs. Thompson to earth.

He never dremt that they were hot upon the trail of Charles Peace, the murderer of Mr. Dyson.

The game was up. The pitcher had gone to the well once too often.

The story of Peace's identification is not the least interesting part of his life, for it illustrates in a striking manner a criminal trait which is so well known that one looks for it in dealing with the history of every criminal.

Peace had made the same sort of mistake that all criminals do sooner or later.

Having absolutely refused to disclose anything about himself, he unwittingly put the police on the track of his identity by writing the letter to Brion.

Inspector Phillips, of the Criminal Investigation Department— then not long in existence—at once went down to Brion's house.

The next day Brion was taken to see the half-caste Ward, whom he had no difficulty in recognising as his old friend, John Thompson.

Back went the police to Evelina Road, but the birds had flown.

Sue Thompson was not one for losing time.

As soon as she heard about the arrest of the half-caste, she knew that the long arm of the law had at last reached the man who had guarded her so closely up to now.

In order to shield herself she set about destroying everything in the house which could possibly give the show away. Some things, such as skeleton keys, she put into a box and threw into the river.

Then the little family party broke up.

Willie Ward was the first to go. He took refuge with his relative, Bolsover, who was still living at Darnall. By-and-by, the remainder of the family arrived.

After selling some of the household effects, and leaving some with Mr. Brion, Sue Thompson and Hannah Ward had their personal effects taken to the railway station, and disappeared.

When Peace was brought up at the police court for the third time and sent for trial, the authorities were ignorant of the value of their prize.

Inspector Bonny said Ward had been seen by many warders and police officers, but nothing could be ascertained concerning him. All they knew was that when he was searched at the police station he had in his possession a pocket-knife which had since been recognised as part of the proceeds of a burglary.

The only thing to be done was to trace Mrs. Thompson. A box the woman had taken to the station with her provided the police with a clue. They followed it up and——

The clue took them to the door of a house in Attercliffe, near Sheffield, once occupied by Charles Peace, the much-wanted Banner Cross murderer.

A Sheffield constable was at once sent up to London in order to identify the prisoner Ward, alias Thompson, and perhaps Peace.

One fine morning a dozen prisoners were turned into the gaol yard and ordered to march round it in single file.

Amongst them was the half-caste, now growing mysteriously white.

Whilst the prisoners marched, the Sheffield policeman watched them.

Suddenly pointing to Peace he exclaimed:

"There he is. That's the man."

Peace saw and heard.

Stepping boldly out of the ranks, his face flushed with anger, he went to the constable and said: "What do you want with me?"

"Get back into the file at once," said the governor by way of reply, and Peace resumed his marching.

On November 6th, 1878, it was announced that Charles Peace had been captured.

The long chase was at an end.

CHAPTER XVII.

Peace Stories Told After the Arrest.

Peace is in prison. He is fairly caught at last. Now, one might reasonably think, has the end of the exciting part of his career been reached.

As a matter of fact, the very reverse is the case. It was when the

THE LIFE STORY OF CHARLES PEACE

burglar and murderer was safe in prison that the newspapers became filled day by day with accounts of his previous doings, as astonishing as they were true.

Here, for instance, is a cutting from the "Daily Telegraph," of November 13th, 1878. Even today, knowing the man's personality as we do, we cannot read it through without a thrill of the most hopelessly mixed feelings.

Then fancy how the disclosures that began to pour in on the public from this date onwards for the next three months must have stirred up the minds of contemporary readers.

"Daily Telegraph," November 13th, 1878:

"The Sheffield murderer. Further disclosures.

"It is now established beyond all doubt that the burglar, captured by Police-constable Robinson is one and the same as the Banner Cross murderer.

"Numerous articles found in the houses of Peace's relatives have been identified by the owners from whose premises they were stolen during the last two years. A large number still remain unclaimed, amongst which is a memorandum tablet in ivory and silver with a silver pencil-case, on the interior of which is inscribed in a writing said to be that of Peace——

"'Miss J. A. Peace. Given to her by her beloved father on her seventeenth birthday; given by Charles Peace.'

"Upon one side, in the same writing, are the words—

"'There is a flower, a gentle flower, that blooms in each shaded spot,
"'And gently to the heart it speaks—forget me not.
"'Love.'

"There are a large number of pawn-tickets for articles—mostly found at Nottingham—the articles being pawned in the name of Thompson, some half-dozen of the tickets being dated after the arrest of Peace.

"The articles pledged include two flutinas, a guitar, two oil-paintings, the aggregate amount advanced on which—including other minor articles—was £3. 13s. 9d.

"The articles remaining to be identified include a cornelian snuff-box, a ramshorn snuff-box with cairngorm set in silver mount, dagger with carved ivory handle in leather case, and some articles of jewellery. The collection is completed by a number of violins, banjos, guitars, and a couple of Aeolian harps.

"A serious jewel robbery took place at Sheffield four years ago, a leading establishment in one of the principal thoroughfares being entered and stripped of £800 worth of goods. The robbery remained a mystery, but there are evidences that it was part of Peace's handiwork."

Truly a remarkable news paragraph, if ever there was one, inasmuch as it shows up clearly practically all of the murderer's most salient characteristics.

Firstly, we have his kindness to his children—for, whatever may be said against him, it is a fact he was kind to them, and a good father in a way. And here it will be noticed that besides Willie, his adopted son, Hannah "Peace" had presented him with a daughter of his own. Coupled with this, we see brought out in striking relief both his love of poetry and of flowers.

Passing from this to the enumeration of stolen and pledged articles, we shall find on a moment's consideration that the list only serves to further show the man's love of the artistic.

Who else but a born artist would trouble to burden himself with objects of purely æsthetic value, such as antique snuff-boxes and oil-paintings of all things, when out on a burgling raid? Besides, the price realised for the first-mentioned of the articles shows clearly enough how bad an investment they would be from the housebreaker's point of view—what with their weight and their trivial selling value. And Peace was not the man to carry off trash through a blind mistake of judgment.

Then we see his intense love of music in the enormous number of musical instruments he annexed. Just think of the danger a burglar would have to run in making his way from a house with a bulky violin-case under his arm.

Yet it is said, and with every show of truth, that Peace never set eyes on a decent fiddle in any house he entered without annexing it forthwith.

Lastly, we have the somewhat veiled allusion to the jewellery robbery.

Not much more about that appeared in the papers, for a very good reason. It would not have done the shop in question any good for it to have published its connection with an episode in the life of the Banner Cross murderer. The customers of a first-class jeweller are not of the sort to put up with advertisements of the firms they patronise gained through the avenue of the police intelligence.

For that same reason, late in the day as it is, we still forbear to mention the name of the jeweller in so many words, though those who reside in or near Sheffield may perhaps be able to guess it.

As to the details of the robbery, however, no such reticence is called for.

Peace had spotted the shop and had laid his plans for some time before a suitable opportunity occurred to bring off the haul. Day after day he watched his chance, and day after day it seemed to grow more remote. Scarcely an hour's vigil did he keep in the guise of the one-armed man without learning something that made his task appear harder than before.

Once, for instance, he had actually settled on the very night for bringing off the coup when he found out by pure chance that the junior partner of the firm was in the habit of sleeping in the shop with a loaded revolver handy by his side. Also a bulldog was kept chained up in the little yard behind within easy earshot to give the alarm in case a would-be burglar should make his appearance.

Needless to say, the visitation to the jewellers was hastily postponed for the time being.

How Peace eventually effected his purpose was in this wise:

It was on a dry but cloudy night in the early part of November, 1874, after it was dark and shortly before closing-time, that a well-dressed and important-looking little man entered the jewellers' and inquired for the senior partner. At the same time he offered his card, which showed him to be the representative of a firm of London office-furnishers, well known and well respected in Sheffield.

"Oh, yes, certainly, the senior partner will see him. Will he come this way?" He is shown into the chief's private office.

Does he start to rifle the safe or look for valuables among the papers on the desk? Not he. Instead, he sits quietly in the chair that has been placed for him, and presently the great man himself arrives.

"Good evening to you. You must excuse my being somewhat late in my call, but the fact is we are pushing the invention I am about to introduce to your notice all we can, and I simply haven't had the time to get here before."

The traveller, otherwise Charles Peace, opens the neat handbag he has brought with him and takes from it a complicated looking arrangement of wires.

"What is it?" The senior partner doesn't understand.

Peace elevates his eyebrows. What, not heard about the new electric burglar alarm? Well, perhaps after all, that is not so surprising.

Now to fully appreciate Peace's cunning and the marvellous originality which he brought to bear upon this most successful robbery it is necessary to remember that at the time when this incident occurred electricity was in its infancy.

The electric light had only been seen by the privileged few in the shape of a scientific experiment. Electric bells were no more generally known. The very idea of utilising the strange power as a protection against housebreakers came to the worthy shopkeeper as a complete novelty.

What wonder then if he needed convincing before he agreed to discard the old precautions in favour of the new.

"But, my good sir, we are as safe as safe can be. Who's going to break in here? You don't know the precautions we take."

"No," agreed Peace, "I do not, but I know what precautions are usual in such cases. They are—" and Peace proceeded to reel off a few of the obstacles he had come up against in the course of his nefarious calling.

To his delight, the senior partner took the bait. Soon he was describing to the "traveller" just how the safeguards adopted at that particular shop differed from those generally in use, and in what way they were superior.

At the conclusion of it all Peace, who had listened with the air of an expert, which, indeed, he was, pointed out one or two weak spots in the shop's fortifications, and straightway demanded to be shown the various protective devices with which the shop was fitted and which had been enumerated to him.

Would you believe it, when just before closing time he sallied forth into the street with his handbag in his hand, he carried in his pocket the senior partner's signed order for six of the new burglar alarms to be fitted on his premises.

Later on he returned to the shop to carry out, not the firm's order, but his own. All was silent now. Within, the lights were extinguished, save only a solitary flickering gas-jet that lit up the front shop. There under the counter the junior member of the firm slept with loaded revolver by his side ready for all emergencies.

The future Banner Cross murderer scaled the low wall that gave on to the little yard where the bulldog kept guard, and dropped down by the brute's side.

It did not give the alarm. It did not stir. The traveller in burglar alarms had "inspected" it together with all the rest of the shop defences. Incidentally he had left a tiny morsel of drugged food by its side all unsuspected by his host of a few hours before.

No fear from the dog. Then Peace made for the locked door that gave on to the shop passage. The lock was one of a sort that in the ordinary way would have defied even him to pick. As it was, he had already "inspected" it, with the result that he had in the interim fashioned a skeleton key so near in shape to the real one that he unlocked the portal with but little trouble.

There was a reassuring creak, and the latch went slipping back. Peace's hand was on the door to push it open when he suddenly hesitated.

Stop! What was the third item down on the order he had so lately received? "One electric burglar-alarm to replace bell pull alarm now fixed to door in shop passage." Ah, of course.

A fumbling in the capacious pocket of his coat, and he brought to light a curious instrument. It was nothing but a pair of ordinary, small-sized, wire-cutting pliers, to the handles of which long metal extensions had been fixed.

And now the door is pushed open a tiny crack, just enough in fact to allow of the strange instrument being inserted through the opening.

Up and down the chink it travels till—— Now it has hit on something—a tightly-stretched wire.

THE LIFE STORY OF CHARLES PEACE

A little more fumbling, and then click! The wire is cut through.

Peace pushed open the door and walked boldly into the shop. His feet, encased as they were in rubber goloshes, made not the slightest sound on the well-laid boards.

If only that order for the electric burglar-alarms had come a bit sooner and through some other channel! The burglar sniggered to himself as he thought of it.

And now he is filling his pockets with valuables out of the various jewel racks. Tiepins, rings, brooches, even small silver candlesticks and plated carriage clocks all find their way into either his pockets or that handy bag he has brought with him.

And still never a sound does he make. The junior partner is sleeping under the counter. Well, let him sleep; he is of no account. There will be no noise to wake him.

Nor was there any noise from the beginning to the end of that queerest of all queer burglaries. In the morning the staff assembled to find the young man frantic with apprehension and the jewellery gone.

How had it been taken? Who could tell? The door of the passage was locked again as it had been after shutting up for the night. Even the dog in the yard had recovered from the effects of the drug, and showed no tell-tale signs to give away the secret of the cracksman's entrance.

Only one thing remained to tell of the burglary beside the loss of the valuables, and that was the severed wire of the alarm.

If only the traveller from ——'s, the office furnishers, had called sooner with his new safety device. Never mind, it would be installed now, anyway.

But the days went by and it never was installed. What was more, the firm never acknowledged the receipt of the order.

At last, when the delay had become considerable, the Sheffield jeweller sent a written complaint, to which the following answer was duly received:

"Queen Victoria Street, E. C.

"To Messrs. Blank, Jewellers.

"Dear Sirs,—We have received yours of the 17th inst. duly to hand, but beg to say your complaint leaves us completely in the dark as to its cause.

"In the matter of electric-alarms, which you mention, we would point out we have no such line catalogued amongst our other items of office furniture, nor were we even conversant with the fact that it was proposed to use electricity in any such way.

"Further, our traveller has not called on you to the best of our knowledge since last March, though we have now given him special instructions to do so when next in Sheffield.—We are, yours, &c."

Let us draw a veil over the feelings of the senior partner when he received that. Little wonder he did not want such a story to go the rounds of the town. Few of us would have cared for it either if we found ourselves in his place.

The foregoing account has the additional merit of being a very fair sample of the type of "Peace story" that went the rounds after the burglar's arrest.

For all that, there is one other account of the man's doings, one that must not be omitted in this life history, since it shows up the Banner Cross murderer in a new and better aspect than any he has been seen in up to now.

The facts about to be recounted only came to light well after Peace's execution.

CHAPTER XVIII.

Peace: Possibilities and Might-have-beens.

Peace was out on burglary bent. It was one of his "all night" nights.

First one business house, then another! Over his arm a suspiciously voluminous coat, under the coat a small sack.

In his pockets skeleton keys, telescopic jemmy, screws for fastening up windows and doors to avoid untimely interruption when engaged in his fell work. In fact, Peace the burglar from the crown of his head to the toes of his boots. Peace the cunning cracksman, the habitual criminal out on the loose, the gaol-bird in the midst of his unholy midnight flittings into every nook and cranny where he had no business to be.

Already his night had brought him luck. The town that was to wake next morning to the realisation of his depredations was Leeds— Leeds within an easy walk of the site of the scaffold on which in due time he was—

"To die a death of shame, on a day of dark disgrace;
To have a noose about his neck and a cloth before his face,
To fall feet foremost through the floor into an empty space."

Light-heartedly the burglar swung round the corner of the very street the continuation of which led to Armley Gaol, to espy, down a turning right opposite to him, a house on fire.

A house on fire! It is a common enough sight—too common by half. And this was only a rickety structure in a dirty little side turning. Nothing to call forth one's interest or cause one to pause, you might well urge.

Yet we do pause when we see a house on fire. And what was more, Peace did so, too. He did more than that. He did exactly what you or I would have done. He forgot for the moment about the business he was on and walked down that side alley to get a better view of all that was taking place.

Soon he found himself on the outskirts of a small but rapidly-gathering crowd of men and women who had turned out of their houses in more or less undress—for it was well after midnight—to see the conflagration.

The crowd was being held back from the front of the burning building by a thin half circle consisting of half a dozen policemen. These had run hastily from their beats to keep the sightseers outside the danger zone, where hot bricks and burning window sashes were already beginning to crash down.

Just as Peace came on the scene a man appeared in the doorway bearing on his shoulder a fainting woman.

One moment! She was out in safety now. A hoarse shout rose for her rescuer while a constable knelt by her side and administered a restorative to her from a flask he carried in readiness for similar emergencies.

A pause, and then she opened her eyes. She was struggling, trying to rise, stretching out her arms to the angry flames that had already begun to play around the upper windows. She was screaming, at first incoherently.

What was it she was screaming about? The crowd pressed round to try to make but head or tail of her ravings.

The blue-coated constables were pressing back the crowd roughly enough, yet with only one thought in their minds, of preserving the eagerly surging throng from danger. For already the beam supporting the roof was beginning to take fire. Presently the roof itself would fall, and—

Bad luck to whoever should be in the way of the falling debris.

And then the woman's words became clearer. Someone nearer to her than the rest heard and grasped her meaning.

What was that whisper going around which stayed the cheering on the lips of the multitude? A child, her only child, still in the building? A widow, and her only child for whom she had worked and starved for nine long years, still in the doomed building?

Someone took a couple of steps toward the door of the house. It was the same scorched, soot-stained man who had rescued the woman. He was one of the right sort, and another cheer went up for him even when after a valiant attempt to make a second entrance he was forced to emerge from the doorway again, stumbling, half suffocated, conquered by the roaring furnace within.

"Here, guv'nor, hold that for me, and mind you keep it safe. It's valuable."

Charles Peace thrust the coat he was carrying, likewise the bag of valuables underneath, into the nearest constable's hand as he stepped bravely forward to make his bid for the life of the otherwise doomed child.

In silence the policeman took charge of the burglar's haul. Had it been anyone else who had volunteered for the forlorn hope it is probable he would have tried to stop him, but not this man with the protruding jaw and the fiercely burning eyes!

"HERE, GUV'NOR, HOLD THAT FOR ME."

In silence, then, he held the sack. In silence the people round about watched the volunteer as he made for the now flaming entrance.

At the door Peace paused to tie a muffler tightly round his mouth and nose. Then he took off his coat and threw it on the ground. As it fell it gave forth a hard, metallic clatter. No one noticed it.

A telescopic jemmy and a bunch of skeleton keys fell out on to the pavement. No one noticed that either.

Then Charles Peace went in.

Who shall say what he endured in that flaming inferno? Who can tell the racking torture through which he supported himself as, with scorched hands and charred finger-nails, he fought his way up the blazing staircase, clinging for dear life to the red-hot bricks of the wall, and leaping with perhaps a prayer, perhaps a curse, on his lips when stairboard after stairboard gave beneath his tread? But what we can set forth here is just the bare fact—and how bare a fact in face of all he must have endured to accomplish it—that after what seemed to the waiting crowd like an eternity, a staggering man garbed in smouldering apparel was seen framed in the casement of the topmost window. In his arms was a white, unconscious burden, while round about his head the smoke and sparks poured forth in a sort of mocking halo.

"Jump! Man, for your life, jump! The roof is falling."

Underneath, willing hands are stretching taut a blanket. Overhead Peace can hear the rotten, flame-scorched timbers parting in a series of sullen, rumbling jars. Yet he waits a second to cast the child into safety before he himself takes the plunge into space that is to snatch him from the very jaws of the licking flame, from the falling roof as it thunders down with a crash like the crash of doom.

He is hurt! He is unconscious! No, he is up and standing on his feet.

Great Scott! What manner of man is this that can walk steadily over to the police-constable and demand "his property" with the red raw marks on face and hands that show him to have been half-roasted alive?

But he sticks to his point. "No, guv'nor, I'm all right. Yes, I'll have a cab if you like to call one, and put my property inside it. And be very careful of it, remember, as I told you it was valuable. What? My name and address? Oh, come, you aren't going to trouble me for that now, are you, when you see the condition I'm in?"

While the constable protests he only wanted it so that the unknown man's brave act should not go without reward, Peace finds himself and his unlawful gains lifted tenderly into the hastily-summoned conveyance.

Just as the cab disappears from before the faces of the astounded spectators the fire engine is heard in the distance rattling up as usual when it is too late to do any good. But don't forget all this is in the seventies, not to-day.

Peace's burns kept him indoors and out of harm's way—or should it be out of the way of inflicting harm on others?—for well over a month. Then he went back to burgling just as though he had not performed an act which had he but followed it with right living would have justly earned for him the name of hero.

CHAPTER XIX.

Ex-detective Parrock Speaks.

NOTE.—*This chapter is of unique interest, as being the contribution of one having in all probability a more intimate knowledge of the Banner Cross murderer than any other living man, namely, Ex-detective Parrock, formerly of the Staffordshire, Yorkshire, and Metropolitan Police Force.*

What do I know of Charles Peace? I should say there are few people, if any, living, who know more of the man than I do.

True, I did not have the luck to capture him. That great honour, and the large monetary collections that followed, went to Constable Robinson, but he is dead. And even were he alive it is doubtful if he could have told so much of Peace's character as I can.

In the old Sheffield days, before the murder of Mr. Dyson, I have fallen in with Peace scores of times. At that time he was known as a doubtful character who required watching.

I remember particularly several occasions when I fell in with Peace at Chesterfield railway station. My duty would take me there, generally to attend the assizes.

I can remember like yesterday how he would sit all hunched up in the corner of the carriage, with his head, which seemed too large for his body, lopping over on to one shoulder. Poor fellow, he must have been misshapen from birth, leave alone the injury to hand and leg which came to him in early youth. I often felt sorry for him as I watched him.

For all that, he could be the best of company. Indeed, when we got into the same compartment with him we did it for him to amuse us, and we were never disappointed.

"Charlie," we would say when the train had started, "we want you to play us some of your latest tunes. Give us a good old operatic selection."

Just one glance would he give at the plain-clothes constables and detectives who surrounded him on all sides, then, without a tremor, and generally with a smile of pleasure, he would comply.

By a curious twist of his elastic mouth he would bring his jaws into a peculiar form, incidentally disclosing a very full and perfect set of teeth. Then, laying back in the carriage, he would bring out a succession of distinct and harmonious notes by striking his teeth with the fingers of either hand.

In this strange manner I have heard him play such difficult selections as those from "Faust" and "Il Trovatore" through from beginning to end, and never once could I detect a mistake or false note.

Sometimes he would vary the performance by playing tunes on a piece of knotted string held between his teeth.

At such times as this my mates and I have talked to him freely. He was always polite in conversation and quite fearless in his attitude towards us. Then, as likely as not, scarcely would he have left our company than the musician would turn into the burglar.

We should receive a hasty summons, perhaps that very night, to go to the scene of some new robbery of his.

And he was a demon of a robber, too. I remember on one occasion not so long after having quite a friendly conversation with Peace being called to track him after the perpetration of no fewer than four robberies in one single night.

This was the occasion when he burgled Abbeydale Hall, Beauchief Hall, Norton Hall, and a farm bailiff's house, all between sunset and sunrise.

We could tell it was he who was responsible for the robberies chiefly by the particular and very skilful way in which he had made entrance through the windows of the various houses. All the same, we didn't catch him. What's more, I for one never did, though twice I actually came within an ace of doing so.

The time I will tell you about first was once when I was attending a flower show in Derby. Just as I was leaving the grounds my attention was attracted by a queer-looking man on the other side of the way.

At once I spotted him as Charles Peace by his walk, though as I was behind him, his face was hidden from me. I decided to get a view of his face before effecting his arrest.

I tried to effect my purpose in every conceivable way, walking first on one side of the road, then on the other, whichever I judged would render me least in evidence and at the same time give the best chance of my seeing him from the front. Two or three times I made desperate efforts to get in front of him while yet not attracting his notice.

It was no use. Although I am quite positive Peace did not know he was being followed, his old habit of being ever on the alert stood him in such good stead that do what I might I never managed to come up with him. And all the while he was making straight towards the market-place where was a great crowd and confusion.

I had begun to realise the affair was becoming desperate, what with the crowds of people which now lined the streets, so I broke into a silent run, determined now to see him face to face at all costs.

Just then he turned his head for an instant. For the moment I distinctly saw Peace before me. The next, a thing happened which I must candidly confess I would not have believed had I not seen it with my own eyes.

The man took to his heels and bolted. At the same time he suddenly straightened himself out, and his whole figure underwent a change right before my very eyes.

It was as though at one instant I was chasing Peace—the next I was after a complete stranger. I found myself following a young man, upright and sprightly. I even believe that at the moment the criminal had in some marvellous manner laid aside the limp which was his distinguishing feature at all other periods of his life.

After that the chase came to an abrupt and unsatisfactory termination. Peace dodged into the centre of a huge mass of sightseers, who had been attracted to the town by the flower show, and on trying to pursue him it soon became evident he had got clear away.

To say I was startled at the sudden change I had witnessed is to put things very mildly. The thing was much too like a miracle to be taken as part of a day's work.

If it were not for the fact that several members of both police and public can testify to having seen the burglar undergo a similar quick change before their eyes, it is doubtful if I should feel comfortable in laying claim to the above experience.

There is the second occasion when I nearly got him to be related, and I must not forget it when the time comes. But before I go on to that I should like to say a few more words about the man as I knew him prior to the Dyson tragedy that put a price on his head, and also as he was known to a friend of mine who used to live only two doors from him at Evelina Road, Peckham.

I have spoken of his wonderful ways of bringing music from the most unlikely objects. I should like to tell you of one more. It is particularly interesting as it shows the way he was occupied on the very afternoon before he shot Mrs. Dyson's husband.

Let me say that Peace was in no sense a drunkard. He would never go in for solitary bouts of drinking. The worst that can be said of him in this matter is that his skill as a musician used to procure for him unlimited treating to free drinks, with the result that occasionally he would leave the local public-house at Eccleshall slightly fuddled and quarrelsome.

The afternoon that preceded the shooting was one on which this was the case, and the reason of it was not far to seek.

That day he had been exhibiting to the occupants of the taproom one of his queerest devices for making music. It was done this way.

First he borrowed from the landlord a long length of stout string. This he stretched right across the room at a height of about six feet from the floor.

Next he got the "potter" (the local name for a very large-sized poker) from the grate. This he tied to the tightly-stretched string so that it hung down in the middle of the room.

Lastly, after a preliminary drink to hearten him up for the work, he took a short stick and began to beat the poker with a series of rapid and curious strokes.

Each stroke brought forth from the suspended poker a musical note, while every stroke seemed to bring out a different one. I have attempted to do the same thing myself, and seen scores of other people try with the same stick and the same poker, in all cases without success. Yet in Peace's hands tune after tune was brought forth to the delight of the assembled company.

This time it was not classical music that was wanted. The folk in the taproom wanted dances, and they got them. Soon they were going round, hopping about and dancing for all they were worth to the strange music. Of course, the musician was not forgotten, and of course his recognition took the usual form of liquid refreshment.

Is it wonderful if, when at last the merriment came to an end, Peace left the place with a heavy head and a fit of the blues that a visit to the clergyman's house only served to augment?

You have heard already how he was coldly received there, and eventually shown the door. Perhaps it is not necessary for me to back up that statement, though, of course, it is true, and was the common talk of the village just after the tragedy.

Peace was not given the chance of working off his ill-humour in harmless words—more the pity. He was treated as of little account. Yet there was to be a time when things were to be very different with him.

For instance, my friend who lived near to him at Peckham, as I have told you, remembers him to this day as a somewhat awe-inspiring person.

Mr. Thompson is the name under which you have heard of his masquerading at Peckham in this account of his life. My friend remembers him as "Colonel Thompson," and by no means a man to be trifled with. I believe he was honestly afraid of the finely-dressed old gentleman who used to stroll by his front door on the rather rare occasions when he went out to take the air in the daytime.

It must have been at the very time that "Colonel Thompson" was doing the grand in Peckham that I had my last brush with Charles Peace on the steps of Holborn Viaduct. And now, I think, is the place to tell you just what happened on that occasion.

I was coming down Farringdon Road chatting with Detective Meiklejohn. You may perhaps remember Meiklejohn's name as that of one of the three detectives afterwards sentenced at the Old Bailey in November, 1877, for conspiracy to defeat the ends of justice—a trial at which Peace was an interested, though, needless to say, unrecognised spectator. All the same, I am not ashamed of owning I was a friend of his at the time of which I speak.

Just as the two of us reached the corner where the stairs start to ascend to Holborn Viaduct we said "Good day!" and parted.

Almost at the same moment I was conscious of someone or something shooting past me and up the stairway.

Alert and suspicious, I turned on the instant just in time to see Peace vanishing round the bend ere I dashed after him, leaping up two stairs at a time.

It was a breathless race between the two of us. The man I was following was agile as a wild cat, yet for the moment I felt sure I had him.

Half-way up the stairs I saw I had gained on him considerably. He was now well in view, and for all my haste I could have sworn to him even then. But I was to come nearer to him still.

Up I dashed. As I watched my quarry Peace increased his pace. I did likewise and managed to keep up with him somehow, though how is a mystery to me to this day. We must have been fairly flying as the end of the stairway was neared.

Now Peace's left foot was on the second step, while his right was on the first step level with the curb of the pavement, while I was on the fifth step, only three clear steps away.

Then I jumped. As I did so my hands flashed out in a wild grab at his flying coat-tails.

I could have sworn I had him. Yet he slipped through my fingers at the last moment. It was Fate, nothing less, which brought about my failure.

I slipped on a fruit skin at the very instant I thought I had him in my grasp.

Down I went on hands and knees, and there to all intents and purposes the chase ended, though I was up again at once and after him at top speed once more.

I remember only too well (how should I forget?) one moment seeing Peace bounding along in front of me, the next he was gone!

That time I honestly could not say whether he effected his strange disappearance by changing his identity before my eyes, as he had already done on two former occasions, or whether he slipped down a side turning unknown to me, or in at the door of some unsuspected empty house.

He was gone. That was all I knew or do know to this day for that matter. I never saw him after that, nor shall I ever discover how he contrived to vanish as he did till the end of my life.

And now a word or two as to Peace's character.

As a man Peace was by no means without good. He was not a man to do another a clandestine injury.

Self-preservation is, as we all know, a first law of nature, and in many of what were painted up at the time as his blackest deeds, he was no more than following out the precept as it applies to one of his evil calling.

Yet he was ever a fair fighter. Those who would make out he was a sneaking coward do him a sad wrong.

THE LIFE STORY OF CHARLES PEACE

He fired often at those who were trying to effect his capture, yet never without fair warning. Even then out of dozens of shots discharged, only three are known to have taken serious effect, of which two bore fatal results.

Yet Peace was a dead shot. There is not a question but that had he wished he could have killed his man every time. Accordingly, the question crops up naturally enough, is it not at least probable that it is the murders he committed which were accidental, not the numerous occasions when he failed to do injury?

At home Peace was never known to be cruel in the way most ill-mated men are cruel to their wives. He never whipped or beat Sue Thompson, openly at any rate, nor did he turn her out of doors as so many evil men would have done, for all she was no more than a public-house sot.

Peace never fired to kill; but more than that can be said of him. As a member of the police I am in a position to say that never once when being apprehended was he known to kick a constable nor to strike from behind.

At the time when Dyson met his death Peace had twice warned him to keep back, both warnings going unheeded. Finally, I may say there is every reason to believe that the actually fatal shot was fired over the burglar's shoulder, a position in which accurate aim would, of course, be quite impossible.

To the neighbours Peace was known as a rather awe-inspiring but for all that kind and sympathetic man. People would go to him in trouble, and seldom would they be sent empty away.

Would that Peace could have met with a like treatment in his early youth, instead of which——

Well, you have read already how he was brought up. In my opinion he never had a chance.

If you want my candid opinion of him as he was, he was a burglar to the backbone, but not a murderer at heart. He deserved the fate that came to him as little as any who in modern times have met with a like one.

And if he had only had a chance at the start of his life, then who can tell what he might have been?

At any rate, I do not for one moment believe he would have ever become what he was—the greatest criminal of the nineteenth century.

CHAPTER XX.

What the Police and the Newspapers Did.

So much for Peace as a man. Is it necessary to say that with the news of his arrest by Police-constable Robinson and subsequent indictment for robbery with violence popular interest was aroused to its uttermost?

In the words of the daily papers, public excitement was intense.

The police were overwhelmed with evidence. From all parts of the country came allegations connecting Peace's name with hundreds of burglaries. If fame was the man's ambition—and the soul of every man thirsts for it—he had certainly attained his goal.

Patchwork accounts of his burglarious exploits spring up like magic in the pages of magazines and newspapers, together with an outpouring of venom such as few politicians have been popular enough to draw from antagonistic party journals.

Every single journal seems to have taken up the tarring and feathering process from the "Times" to the "Police News." One and all were universal in dubbing the caged burglar as big a coward and bully as he was undoubtedly a rogue. According to such accounts he was not only a hardened murderer, but also quite the most callous and brutal one that had ever existed. Indeed, in face of such a vituperation throughout the whole of the public press there is little wonder that the man has gone down to posterity as a black-hearted scoundrel.

No wonder in face of all the above that police and public alike found solace in baiting him with a mock trial and mock life sentence at a time when they well knew his final condemnation to death was but a matter of weeks.

Even when his fate was practically sealed the public rancour did not abate.

Read this from the "Daily News" of date January 24th, 1879, when everyone knew Peace was already as good as doomed to the gallows.

"The condition of Peace is still causing the greatest uneasiness. During the day he has been supplied with nourishing food, and part of his diet was *mock turtle soup*. The greatest possible attention is being paid to the prisoner."

The paragraph goes on to re-affirm with many grave medical particulars the reasons for the general concern for the health of the convict, who, just two days before, made an unsuccessful attempt at committing suicide. Could anything be more brutal than this thirst to preserve a fellow human being alive until such time as he was ripe for killing?

After the perusal of the above newspaper extract we shall make no apology for asking the reader's attention to this other, which occurs in the issue of three days later, even though, in a way, it may be only going over old ground.

Speaking with regard to the murder of Mr. Dyson on account of which Peace is being thus carefully preserved for hanging, it remarks: "It is a singular fact that the convict on leaving Banner Cross on the night of the murder did not know of the death of Mr. Dyson. In fact, it was not until the following morning, when he read the account of the murder in the newspapers, that he was aware Mr. Dyson was dead. Then he felt it needful to be more careful in his movements, and disguised himself."

But the bitterest pill of all so far as Charles Peace's feelings were concerned must have been the way in which his former friends and associates turned on him in his distress as wolves turn on a maimed brother in the pack.

The depth of hatred that burned up at the mere mention of his name in the heart of the public he could only dimly guess at.

What he could know all too well and feel correspondingly acutely was the way in which his former intimates played Judas over his living body, vying with one another as to the price they could extract from the Government over his condemnation.

You have already heard to a certain degree what sort of woman Sue Thompson was. That she was indeed the traitoress she has been called cannot be made plainer than by the perusal of the two following letters reprinted from the issue of the "Daily Telegraph" bearing the date February 8th, 1879.

The first letter is written by Sue Thompson to Charles Peace while he was lying in Armley Gaol under sentence of death. He had expressed a wish to see her.

> "My Dear John," it ran—referring to Peace in the character of John Thompson—"You have expressed a wish to see me. I shall come down to Leeds to know if I can be admitted, and, if possible, to cheer you up a little. You know what we have been to each other—all in all—until this has befallen you and me who has suffered so greatly.—Darling.
>
> "Yours, SUE."

Next to it comes the reprint of the following letter to "Yours, Sue," emanating from the solicitor to the Treasury:—

> "Reg. v. Peace.   February 6th, 1879.
> "Madam,—
> "Your letter addressed to Mr. Pollard, of this department, asking for the Government reward in this case—£100 for such information as would lead to the conviction, &c.—has been handed to me.
> "I have no authority to deal with your application, which should be made to the Home Office.—Yours obediently,
> "A. K. STEPHENSON,
> "Solicitor to the Treasury.
> "Mrs. S. Bailey, alias Thompson."

Thus it will be seen that the very day after the passing of the death sentence on the man she had called her husband, and almost in the same breath with which she took pen in hand to sign her letter to him, "Ever yours, Sue," she was making application to the Treasury for the reward of one hundred pounds due to her for selling him to the authorities.

On one occasion also the name of Brion has been mentioned as another of Peace's doubtful friends. Brion, it will be remembered, was the neighbour with whom Peace used to discuss and work out his inventions when living at Peckham.

Up to the time when the master criminal was arrested he is credited with having been entirely ignorant as to the former's real nature, as indeed, for all that it is known, he may have been. Yet, whether this was so, or whether he was as great a criminal as the other, there can be no two opinions as to the scurvy way in which he rounded on the whole Peace household in the hope of diverting suspicion from himself by siding openly and before all the world with the custodians of law and order.

A weak standpoint to take, you will doubtless say, yet one to which many an innocent man might have been tempted under like circumstances. Perhaps so; but that does not make it any the more admirable; nor does it go far to smooth over such a piece of minor treachery as is reported of him on the occasion when he paid his final visit to the doomed man in the condemned cell.

On that occasion Peace was discovered by Brion lying shivering on a mass of rugs, trying to find solace for his last hours in the perusal of some devotional work.

As Brion entered, the convict put the book down, and after a few muttered and repentant explanations, came to the main object of his "friend's" visit.

Brion, now that Peace was safe under lock and key, claimed that the inventions which had been patented in the joint names of the two were in reality his alone, Peace having got his name added by undue influence.

This Peace of course denied, at the same time offering to sell his right in them to the other for fifty pounds.

Indignantly Brion declined the offer, reiterating the statement that he had been defrauded by his now helpless former associate.

For answer, Charles Peace, after a short inward struggle, during which time he was composing his mind to the sacrifice, turned to him and said:

"Very well, my friend, let it be as you say. I have not cheated you, Heaven knows, but I also know that this infamy of mine has been the cause of bringing harm to you, which is the last thing I should have wished to have caused to my friend. So, if you can arrange it, I will agree to make you a present of all my share in the inventions, so that you may forgive me for this that I have done to you, and so that you will believe I die truly repentant for my many sins."

Having spoken thus, the chaplain was sent for and the deed of gift set forth in Chapter XII duly drawn up, signed, and handed over to Brion. Then, with further tokens of repentance, the criminal took his final farewell of the one who had been his crony for so many months past.

Brion had scarcely got outside the door of the cell than, turning to the governor, who was by his side, he said:

"You saw all that sham about repentance and finding solace in religion?"

"Yes," said the Governor shortly. "What have you to say about it?"

"Only that if you'll take the opinion of one who knew him well it's all bunkum! Mark my words, he'll have another attempt at breaking away before many days are out. This is only one of his many preparations for escape designed to put the warders off their guard. If I were you I should put a double watch on him."

Needless to say, subsequent facts quite failed to bear out Brion's statement. All along from that time to the day of his execution Peace was an exemplary prisoner; but the account only serves to show one instance of the treachery towards him of those who had so often benefited in the past, and were even then doing so in the present, at his hands.

Perhaps while on this subject it would be interesting to add that Mrs. Brion, working hand and glove with her husband turned herself for the occasion into an amateur detective, making it her business to follow, wherever she went, Sue Thompson, whom they had pressed to accept of free hospitality under their roof.

When Sue went abroad Mrs. Brion would dog her footsteps even as Hannah Ward had done before her. In the end virtue was rewarded. By means of clues obtained in this wise, she was able to disclose to the police the whereabouts of a quantity of silver spoons and forks stolen by Peace and put in pledge by his female accomplice after his arrest.

Finally, it must not be omitted that in due time a heavy bill for the "free hospitality" extended to Mrs. Thompson, also for Brion's energy on the side of right and law, with a substantial addition under the heading, "To time and wages lost," was submitted by the devoted couple to the Treasury and honourably paid.

So much for the friendship of the Brion family.

Beside it even the venom of the gutter press sinks into insignificance.

When not employed in blackening Peace's character, or reporting incidents connected with his trial, the better-class newspapers towards the end of 1878 took to a practice that soon became very popular. This was none other than the recounting of story upon story illustrating the burglar's undoubted and admittedly extraordinary powers of disguise.

They were full of rumours of strange get-ups, some of them as complicated as they would have been futile, which Peace was credited either with having actually adopted or with having had prepared for him to aid him in his escape from the authorities.

One of the latter class is found spoken of in the "Daily News" for January 24th, 1879. We print the paragraph in question as voicing one of the many absurd rumours that went the rounds after Peace's attempted suicide—an event in the burglar's history which will unfold itself further in due course.

"It was rumoured that Peace's leap from the train was part of a plot, that he had secretly arranged with friends to jump out at that exact spot (not far from Darnall), and that a woman had been seen near the line with a bundle of clothes and a set of false whiskers with which to disguise Peace in the event of his escape."

Poor Peace! It seems rather hard on him thus to take away his character for effective concealment of his identity by thrusting on him before the popular gaze a pair of false whiskers at a time when he was unable to adequately refute the libel.

But to return to the police, who, now that the Banner Cross murderer was safe under lock and key, began to think about tracing his supposed accomplices.

Having landed the biggest fish in the net, the authorities now proceeded to whip out the smaller fry, and on November 7th they arrested Hannah Ward at Darnall. They found in the house a number of articles, which were afterwards identified at Blackheath as property that had been stolen. Amongst the booty were a silk dress, a patent clock, five parcels of jewellery, two watches, and an opera-glass.

Meanwhile the police having also succeeded in tracing the whereabouts of Sue Thompson through the agency of Mr. Brion, of whom we have already heard—who had now learned, for the first time, what his old friend Mr. Thompson was—they requested him to keep an eye on her, and she was brought to London, where she soon placed the detectives in possession of all the information they wanted.

One by one Peace's relatives were sought out and questioned.

As for Hannah Ward, she strenuously denied that she knew that the articles found in her house had been stolen. For all that, she was remanded in custody to London soon after her "husband" had been tried and sentenced for shooting at Constable Robinson.

The case was tried by Mr. Justice Hawkins, and Peace had the assistance of Mr. Montagu Williams, the most famous criminal lawyer of his day.

Although Montagu Williams had "restored many a burglar to his friends and his relations," the verdict was a foregone conclusion. The prisoner was found guilty. Asked if he had anything to say, he made the following extraordinary speech—a speech which Charles Peace alone could have made. There is that strange odour of mixed candour and humbug about it that cannot be mistaken. In it, as in so many of his statements made about this time, we seem to see the "was" contending furiously with the "might have been":—

"Yes, I have this to say, my lord," began Peace. "I have not been fairly dealt with, and I declare before God that I never had the intention to kill the prosecutor, and all that I meant to do was to frighten him in order that I might get away. If I had had the intention to kill him, I could easily have done it, but I never had that intention. I declare I did not fire five shots, I only fired four; and I think I can show you, my lord, how I can prove that only four shots were fired. If your lordship will look at the pistol, you will see that it goes off very easily, and the sixth barrel went off on its own accord after I was taken into custody. At the time the fifth shot was fired the constable had hold of my arm, and the pistol went off quite by accident. I really did not know that the pistol was loaded, and I hope, my lord, that you will have mercy on me. I feel that I have disgraced myself. I am not fit either to live or die. I am not prepared to meet my God; but still I feel that my career has been made to appear much worse than it really is. Oh, my lord, do have mercy upon me, and I assure you that you shall never repent it. As you hope for mercy yourself at the hands of the great God, do have mercy on me and give me a chance of redeeming my character and preparing myself to meet my God. I pray and beseech you to have mercy upon me."

Mercy!
Charles Peace knew the execution of English law in the seventies left little enough room for its exercise.

But more, did he only know it, beyond the court, beyond the judge, beyond the world itself, something was outlined against eternity, at which even he shuddered. Those about him already knew what the future would hold in store for the wretched man—a rope dangling over an open grave. . . .

And by the side of the grave Death mocking him.

* * * * * *

He awoke from his own reflections to the cold, measured phrases of the judge.

He caught the words, "Accomplished burglar . . . a man who would not hesitate to commit murder . . . the extreme sentence of the law. . . . natural life."

His heart withered and turned to stone.
His punishment was worse than death.

CHAPTER XXI.

Peace's Last Adventure.

On January 14th, 1879, Hannah Ward was discharged, after trial at the Old Bailey, on the technical ground that being the "wife" of

PEACE HAD TO BE LITERALLY FORCED INTO THE COMPARTMENT.

Page 109.

THE LIFE STORY OF CHARLES PEACE

Peace she had acted under his coercion and could not therefore be held responsible for any criminal act.

Three days later Peace was taken to Sheffield to be charged with the murder of Mr. Dyson.

After a long search the police had traced Mrs. Dyson to America, and on January 6th she arrived at Sheffield.

At the start of the police-court inquiry Peace seems to have made the most of his new liberty of speech after the silence of solitary confinement.

He complained about the injustice with which he was being treated. He told the magistrates that if they did not want him to speak they would have to put a gag in his mouth.

Remonstrated with, he replied that he was not a dog.

"I shall interrupt the Court as often as I like," he said, "because I am determined to have justice done to me."

Certainly a perusal of the newspaper reports of the proceedings leaves one with the impression that the authorities were by no means so anxious on that point.

The case was adjourned, and the master criminal was taken back to London. On Wednesday, January 23rd, he was put into the train again and taken to Sheffield. That journey will live in criminal history, for it provided an unparalleled sensation—the escape and recapture of Charles Peace.

On the journey from Sheffield to London after the first remand he gave the warders who travelled with him no end of anxiety.

Having been allowed to leave the train at Peterborough, he refused to enter it. A large crowd collected on the platform, and so desperate was Peace's resistance that he had to be literally forced into the compartment.

It was on his return journey to Sheffield that he made his last fight for freedom. And what a terrible fight it was.

On the morning of the 22nd Peace was to appear before the magistrates. The scene in and around the court was extraordinary.

The early morning trains brought thousands of people from all parts of the Midlands, and the doors of the court were soon besieged by a mob big enough to sack the city.

Nine o'clock struck.

The magistrates were ready. Everyone in court was on the tiptoe of expectation.

The hands of the clock crept on to the quarter, but there was no sign of the prisoner. What had happened?

Suddenly the busy hum of conversation ceased just as a man ceases to talk when he is shot dead.

Instead of the magistrates, the Chief Constable, Mr. Jackson, slowly walked on to the bench. He seemed to be strangely agitated.

"Gentlemen," he said, "I am sorry to say—there is nothing to be heard to-day—Peace—has—escaped! At least, that is what I hear; but you had better wait and see what may happen."

Peace escaped!

Solicitors, barristers, witnesses, and spectators all sat bolt upright in their seats, numbed, petrified.

Peace escaped!

Yes, it was true. A roar of excitement in the street outside seemed to confirm the incredible news.

At half-past eight everything should have been ready for the hearing.

The prisoner was "on his way." He "would arrive" in a moment.

An inspector went down to the railway-station to meet the train due in at 8:45.

He found in it neither Peace nor the warders—instead, in an empty compartment there were a warder's cutlass and a bag of papers.

According to the guard, the prisoner had managed to jump from the train and the warders had gone in pursuit.

The inspector hurried back to the Town Hall, where the Chief Constable was awaiting the arrival of the prisoner.

All that he could gasp out was, "Escaped! Escaped!"

"From you?" yelled the Chief.

"No—from the London—men!"

What was to be done?

It was as if some national catastrophe had been announced.

The Chief Constable hurried to the windows of the Town Hall and addressed the crowd.

When he told them that Peace had escaped there was a deep groan of disappointment.

But at that very moment a message was put into his hand, and he announced, amidst bursts of frantic cheering, that the convict had been recaptured, and was at that moment on his way to Sheffield.

At half-past nine there was lifted out of a train into a prison-van a ghastly bundle of bleeding flesh.

Groaning and moaning he was driven to the police-station and laid on a bed in a cell.

The doctor was sent for.

As he entered the cell a head wearily raised itself from the mass of rugs in which it had been concealed——

And Charles Peace, all maimed and torn, asked for a drop of brandy.

They gave it to him, and he sank back into his rugs.

Poor Peace! It was his last adventure.

HE LEAPS FROM AN EXPRESS TRAIN.

The story of what took place in a railway-carriage during the journey from London to Sheffield, after Peace's final arrest, reads more like a piece of popular melodrama than a chapter taken from a real life's history.

From the moment he got into the train Peace was restless. For this there was some reason. The railway-carriages of those days were far less roomy and comfortable than they are now, and corridor trains were unknown.

Little wonder, then, if convicts of those days, like their more fortunate brethren, should have highly valued the privilege usually allowed them of stretching their legs at the stations—under escort, of course.

In the case of Charles Peace, however, the warders in charge of him thought, no doubt rightly, that to let their man out of the carriage for an instant would mean a grave danger of his escaping. Accordingly, they sternly refused him permission to leave it; a decision which put their prisoner in a hugely bad temper.

By way of getting his own back Peace tormented them in a thousand little ways during the journey, eventually offering as a sort of compromise to curtail hostilities if he might be allowed to have the window open.

Incautiously the worried warders granted the request, nor did they suspect what was coming when the convict walked to it and casually put his head out.

The train had now got to a point near Shire Oaks and Kineton Park, not far from Sheffield.

Peace knew every inch of this district.

Very soon the warders had cause to regret their laxness.

Suddenly Peace crouched, and at one terrific bound, shot through the window.

Quick as thought, one of the warders made a grab at him. He was just in time to catch him by the left foot.

The other warder sprang to the communication cord. It failed to act.

The carriage window was so narrow that the second warder was utterly unable to help his comrade.

Whilst the train rushed on Peace hung out over the footboard, struggling like a maddened tiger.

He squirmed and wriggled with diabolical ferocity.

Great beads of perspiration rolled off the warder. His strength was being rapidly exhausted. He was fighting a fiend.

The warder's grip slipped from the foot to the boot, and the boot was coming loose.

Another moment and Peace had wrenched himself free.

The warder fell back in the compartment with the boot in his hand.

Meanwhile the noise of the struggle had prompted a man in an adjoining compartment to put his head out of the window.

The frantic warders told him what had happened. Reaching out with his arm he managed to pull the communication cord.

In another moment the train was stopped.

The warders jumped down and ran back along the line to see what had happened to Peace.

They found him all cut and bleeding lying in a ditch.

Maimed as he was, the extraordinary man was feebly trying to force the handcuffs over his wrists. He even smiled faintly when he saw the warders.

A few moments later Peace was put into the guard's van of a passing train.

"Oh, my poor head! Oh, my poor head!" he kept moaning, as they laid him on a pile of rugs. He said nothing to his captors. He simply lay there beaten and broken.

Luckily—as the public opinion of the time went—he had escaped with no more severe injury than concussion of the brain. But it was a very bad concussion. All the rumour that went about afterwards that Peace was shamming ill effects from his fall was sheer nonsense.

The morning after his recapture a discovery was made which added a second sensation to one that was already overwhelming.

The leap from the train was not, as everyone had thought, an attempt at escape; it was nothing more nor less than a frenzied bid to cheat the executioner by committing suicide.

When the prison officials came to examine his clothes they found in the breast-pocket of his coat a piece of paper on which was scribbled:

> "Bury me at Darnall.
> God bless you all.
>
> CHARLES PEACE."

He actually jumped from the train at a point not far distant from the church at Darnall, and quite close at hand was the house in which he used to live when he was tormenting the Dysons.

One may imagine the terrible duration of the struggle between the warder and Peace when it is said that on an examination of the line being made the convict's spectacles were found about a mile and a half from the point at which he left the train.

Peace himself has left us the following comment on the incident:

> "When the warders brought me down from London to the first examination I took a long look at Darnall. I did the same as they took me back, and after I was locked up in my cell at Pentonville the thought came over me that if I had to go down again I would try to destroy myself. I had seen from the manner in which the warders had guarded me both going down and coming up that I had no chance of escaping, and while I was in my cell I got two pieces of paper, and I pricked on one: 'Bury me at Dar-

nall; God bless you all!' and I found a piece of black something in my cell, and wrote the same thing on the other. My hope was that in jumping from the train I should arrange to fall under the wheels and be cut to pieces. Then I should have been taken to the 'Duke of York,' and there would have been an inquest over me. As soon as the inquest was over you could have claimed my body, and then I should have been buried at Darnall, which was what I wanted."

Can one help wishing Peace had got his way? But the hangman was not to be cheated.

*   *   *   *   *   *

Two days after the attempt to escape from the train the preliminary inquiry was finished and the case was ready to go to trial.

The authorities went so far as to hold the adjourned inquiry in the corridor adjacent to the cells.

Peace was apparently not well enough to stand the strain of an appearance in the police-court. If such was the case, there can be no doubt that the feeling in some quarters after the man's death that the trial had been hurried through with irreverent haste was to a great extent justified.

The only excuse that can be found to justify the hurried preliminary proceedings is that the assizes were to open in a week, and Peace was such a slippery eel that the police were literally afraid to take the responsibility for his detention a moment longer than was necessary. Hence the extraordinary proceedings that took place in the corridor.

In Mrs. Maybrick's case part of the preliminary proceedings were conducted in the prisoner's bedroom. But she was merely being charged.

In Peace's case the police-court side of the business was rushed along as if the hangman were already knocking at the Town Hall doors.

Ill and broken as he was, the convict was half carried, half dragged to the chair in the corridor where the preliminary inquiry was taking place. He practically sank into the bottom of it, and when he spoke his voice seemed to come from somewhere beneath the table.

Once he complained that he was cold, and some rugs were thrown about his shoulders, so that his head was completely buried. That was good enough treatment for the man who had given the police more trouble than anyone else for the last fifty years.

Whilst Mrs. Dyson was giving evidence he tried to conduct his case to the best of his ability, even falling into the mistake of openly supplementing his counsel's endeavours in this respect.

Now it was a witness he wanted called; then some documents he was anxious should be exhibited. Probably his well-meant efforts only went against him if the truth were known.

"Let me go away now," he said at last.

The police-surgeon got up and felt his pulse.

"He'll do very well where he is," he said gruffly, and the magistrate ordered the inquiry to continue. This was at the time the convict was being fed on *mock turtle soup* in the effort to preserve his life for the hangman.

At last the evidence was complete, and he was asked if he had anything to say.

"If you take my advice," said Mr. Clegg, his solicitor, "you will simply say that you are not guilty."

But Peace was smarting too much from his recent rebuffs to be advised.

"I say I am not guilty," said he; "and I say that I have not had justice done to me to prove that I am not guilty. There is a lot of witnesses, and I can say that I can prove that that base, bad woman threatened her life and his life. But"—impatiently—"I cannot talk to you; I am so bad."

Having made this statement, Peace signed it.

Rambling as it is, one cannot help seeing in it all the pathos linked up with a warped disordered brain led by the blind instinct of self-preservation.

Upon being taken back in his cell Peace seemed to revive. He was treated as if he had already been condemned, that is to say, two warders were always in the cell to watch him. There seemed to be an unholy fear that somehow or other he would cheat the gallows.

He was never allowed to put his head under the bed-clothes at night. He was compelled to sleep with his arms and hands in view. The authorities even put his spectacles out of his reach when he was not using them, for fear that he would do himself some injury with the rims.

Perturbed by all these precautions? At any rate he did not show it. Perhaps he even derived a grim satisfaction from them. Looked at from one point of view, they were tributes to his former prowess.

Laid on his pallet, he waited patiently while the days slipped by to the time of his trial. Sometimes he would occupy himself by recounting his exploits to the warders who stood about him. But every now and then the head with its ferrety eyes would pop cautiously out of the blankets and peer round as though by force of long habit.

There were to be no more opportunities for Charles Peace. The warders watched him like lynxes.

Morning came, and with it Mr. Hallam, the police-surgeon, who certified that the convict was fit to be moved. Having handcuffed him, some officers carried him down to the parade-ground, where the police-van was waiting to take him to the railway station.

On the way down the stairs Peace moaned uneasily. He was still far from well. Indeed, he had not completely recovered his strength at the time of his execution. "Where am I going to?" he asked. "Where are you taking me to?"

"You're going to Wakefield," was the reply.

Wakefield! He must have thought of the Wakefield he knew many years before. The gallows were not so unpleasantly near in those days, and he had thoughts of making a name for himself. But not a name like this. Ugh!

They put him in the van and covered him up with rugs. The doors were shut with a bang, and off went the dismal equipage to the station. What a progress it was. There was a crowd big enough to delight the heart of a king. Thousands of men and boys clattered after the van as it rumbled through the streets. Inside lay Peace, the central figure of it all, listening dully to the hoarse shouting outside. It sounded like the hungry yelping of a pack of wolves.

In order to escape the mob, the van was quickly driven past the main entrance to the station to a yard further along, where it was hoped that it would be possible to get Peace quietly into the train.

But the crowd detected the manoeuvre. Bursting through the cordon of the police, the people dashed after the van, surged on to the railway line, and literally fought for a glimpse of the prisoner.

Amongst the spectators, holding an informal reception, was Constable Robinson, whom Peace had shot at Blackheath.

The injured convict was soon transferred from the prison-van. The whistle of the engine shrieked, someone waved a flag, and the journey to Peace's final resting-place had commenced.

As the train moved out of the station someone called out:

"Give him a parting cheer. He's a plucky dog!"

The only reply came in the midst of an angry howl.

"Give him a rope rather."

That was the Sheffield of the seventies.

Present-day crowds are seldom so vindictive.

* * * * * *

Wakefield prison at last.

Peace noticed that the place was very much as it was in the old days. He heard the gates shut behind him.

Then the warders stooped down to lift him out as before.

"Put him down," said an inspector brutally. "We're not going to carry such as him."

Weak as Peace was, the prison officials deliberately stood back while he tottered into the grim building that was to be his last earthly abode as best he could.

CHAPTER XXII.

The Great Trial.

On Tuesday, February 4th, 1879, Peace was tried at Leeds by Mr. Justice Lopes, and found guilty of the wilful murder of Arthur Dyson.

There have been many great criminal trials since those far-off days, but it is a question whether there has been anything so sensational, so melodramatic, so crammed with human interest as Peace's last appearance in a court of justice.

All Peace's life the soul of the man had longed for Fame, and now at last Fate had poured him out a full and overflowing measure.

Yet from the spectacular point of view Charles Peace, the prisoner, was popularly voted a disappointment. As might be expected, he failed to come up to the scratch when compared with his portrait on the cover of the "Police News." The imagination of the streets had been fed up with pictures of not merely a daring burglar and an unscrupulous murderer, but also a sort of second Dick Turpin—fine, bold, devil-may-care; such a man as would appear in the dock, cool, jaunty, and debonair to the bitter end.

The man the public actually saw did play his part, and he played it exceedingly well, but it was not the part they were tuned up to. Instead, the tragedy almost became a piece of sloppy sentiment, full of tears and groanings. Peace was not a coward, as his words after sentence had been pronounced would soon show, but he acted the coward now for all he was worth. He was playing for sympathy, the one remaining hope of the convicted murderer.

Here is a picture of the scene:

The great court-house is packed from floor to ceiling. No collection of Dicks and Harrys this, but, if you please, the flower and fashion of the country, ruffled and scented, and flushed with excitement. Not a place this for a woman, but she is everywhere, talking, chattering, playing off her pretty wit in the very presence of death. It is ever the way.

The dock is just a desert island amongst a sea of faces. There is the bench, too, looking like a stage with the curtain down, and the jury-box the empty seats waiting for the orchestra.

At last there is a sign of life in the empty places, as one by one the twelve good men and true solemnly get into their box, where they sit like so many wax figures on show. A moment later and their names are being called out.

A warder comes up into the dock and puts a chair just behind the iron railings. Somebody else puts the books and papers necessary for the occasion on the judge's seat, and then——

"Silence"—and "m'lud" himself is in his place, and the favoured few who are to have seats beside him are shuffling into their chairs with the air of distinguished guests whose privilege it is to come to the theatre late and interrupt the players.

Hush!

Far down beneath the court, as from a tomb, comes the sound of jangling keys and the banging of iron doors.

Three warders tramp up the steps into the dock.

The prisoner is coming—Charles Peace, the terrible man-eating tiger of villainous reputation. The women huddle together like sheep

THE LIFE STORY OF CHARLES PEACE

when the wolf is by. They strain their eyes towards the dock, and they see——

They see a decrepit old man being half dragged, half pushed up the stairs. They drag him up as if he were an unwieldy sack, and dump him down in the chair.

He looks more like a stuffed effigy than a man. His head hangs limply over one shoulder. His feet hardly seem to touch the ground. The pale, sunken face and high cheek-bones look like a death-mask.

A murmur of surprise runs round the court. Is this the great Peace, the terror of a town and the scourge of a whole country? Scores of opera-glasses are turned on him as he sits listless in the dock. On either side of him is a warder. There is another behind, and still further back a whole row of warders is in waiting in case the old fires blaze up and Peace makes trouble.

When the Clerk of Assize asks him to say whether he is guilty or not guilty, he makes shift to rise. But he drops into his seat again like a wet rag and feebly shakes his head.

The first dramatic moment comes when Mrs. Dyson enters the box. She tells the story of the fatal night—but she never looks at the prisoner.

There are faint signs of life in Peace now. He rests his head on his hands, but he supports himself by putting his elbow on the dock-rail. His eyes are riveted on the woman in the witness-box, but he makes no sign, except when she says something which displeases him. Then his jaws begin to work nervously. But that is all.

A new witness takes the woman's place.

It is Police-constable Robinson, the hero of Blackheath.

Hush! Not a word of his story must be lost. Once again the opera-glasses are brought out. A thousand eyes flit from the constable to the limp, prison-clothed figure in the dock. You could hear a pin fall as the deathless story is told again.

And now the day is getting on. They light the gas, and the place is more like a theatre than ever.

And still Peace makes no sign except when in an eloquent speech for the defence his counsel, Mr. Lockwood, exclaims: "I do not deny that he is a wild and reckless man."

There is a mournful shake of the prisoner's head at this.

The old fox may be play-acting, but he knows that the game is up.

At twelve minutes past seven the jury retire in order to consider their verdict, and Peace is taken down below.

In eight minutes—think of it—they return. Peace watches them narrowly, but he can read no sign of hope in their stolid faces. There is nothing there but doom.

Suddenly he starts. . . . "Guilty!"

The Clerk wants to know if he has anything to say.

"Anything to say? . . . What's the use of saying anything?"

Very well, then, the Judge must pass sentence. . . .
He is passing sentence now.
The wretched creature in the dock is being propped up by warders. Listen to the Judge.

"Charles Peace," he says, "after a most patient trial, and after every argument has been put forward by your learned counsel on your behalf which ingenuity could suggest, you have been found guilty of the murder of Arthur Dyson by a jury of your fellow-countrymen. It is not my duty—still less is it my desire—to aggravate your feelings at this moment by recapitulating any portion of the details of what I fear I could only call your criminal career. I implore you to use the short time that remains to you in life in preparing for eternity. I pass upon you the sentence—the only sentence which the law in this case permits, which is that you——"

Peace hears no more. His withered frame sinks beneath him. Another moment and the warders are carrying him out of the dock.
As he goes down out of the sight of his fellow-creatures his voice is feebly raised in supplication:
"Have mercy, O my lord!"
There is the clang of an iron gate and the jangle of keys.

* * * * * *

That is the Charles Peace the public bids farewell to. To them the man is an arrant coward, but his very seeming terror of death forces them to reflect on the horror of the punishment they have passively helped to bring down on him. Had his crimes been less heinous it is even possible that some of the spectators in court might have been worked upon to agitate for a reprieve.

Little would they guess that this was the very thing the convicted man had been working for all the time.

As it is, the spectators realise the man's past is too horrible to think of that. There is no demonstration. They simply get up and leave the court as one would leave a church after a funeral.

For them Charles Peace is dead and buried.

* * * * * *

Once out of sight of the court Peace put foot to floor and walked to the waiting prison-van with firm step.

On his way he turned to his jailer and made the following remark in a quiet, level voice, without a trace of fear or dread in it:—

"Well, I'm a-going to be executed, and I suppose I can't complain, but what I say is this: I'm going to be hung for what I done, but never intended."

The man was acting no longer. Seeing that he has long since paid the fullest penalty for his many crimes, may we not show him the generosity of spirit to take his words as they stand and in good faith?

PEACE SENTENCED TO DEATH.

Page 118.

CHAPTER XXIII.

Peace's Last Days.

After sentence of death had been passed Charles Peace was taken back to Armley Gaol.

When he first arrived the authorities decided to put him in a large cell, so that two warders could always be with him on guard.

The authorities had got into their heads a notion that Peace would defeat the hangman in spite of all the watching in the world. The origin of the idea was a supposed saying of Peace's that he "had that in his head which would do them yet," referring to a supposed trick of his of turning his tongue towards the back of his mouth and "swallowing" it—a well-known Chinese method of suicide.

Almost the first thing Peace did when he got back to his cell after the trial was to write the following letter to his family. It is one of many he penned before his death:—

"I shall do my very best," he says, "to prepare myself to meet my God and to obtain His forgiveness, if it is possible, for the sins of my past life. I hope this will be one consolation and comfort to me—that is, by thinking of my sentence of life-imprisonment before my present sentence of death was passed upon me. You must understand that I should have had a long and dreary and miserable life of imprisonment, for imprisonment is much harder now than it has ever been known, and if I had nothing against my character I should have had to have been twenty years before I could be recommended for my freedom, and even then it would entirely depend upon the merits of the case. So that I think I should never have gained my freedom, but should have died a miserable death on a prison bed, surrounded by a class of men anything but good and God-fearing. Let this be a comfort to you and your family, that I am neither a fool nor an idiot to say we think there is no God. On the contrary, I know there is a merciful God whom I have sinned against and broken all His commandments all the days of my life. I hope and trust that I shall feel that my great load of sins will be forgiven me by His granting me free repentance, and by my blessed Lord and Savior Jesus Christ washing me and cleansing me from my sins and raising my poor soul into the kingdom of Heaven, where I hope to meet you and all my dear family at the last great day. If any people are so mean as to sneer at you because of me, put it down to their badness and take my advice and leave it to their foolishness and God to deal with them."

It is difficult to know how to read such a letter. For a man like Peace to talk about his fellow-convicts as "anything but good and God-fearing" men different from himself was too much like when the pot called the kettle black. Still no one is entitled to say what passed in the soul of the condemned man during the three weeks that elapsed between his sentence and excution. That lies alone between him and his Maker. His prison correspondence goes far to substantiate the belief that within his poor, diseased brain there really lurked more than a glimmer of true religion.

And even if now that Peace's evil life has almost run its course, we cannot find it in ourselves to judge him more mercifully, let us at least remember that somewhere in the blackest of hearts there is always room for an angel.

Mr. Brion, Peace's old partner at Peckham, seems, with all his petty meannesses, to have taken this view, for, writing to him after the trial, he says:

> "I never thought that you were an irreligious man, and even now I believe that had you early confided in a sound, Christian friend you would have left your evil ways and possibly, possessing great abilities as you do, would have made wealth and an honourable position in the world. . . You remember that on Sunday evenings you used to enjoy singing hymns of praise. Notwithstanding all that has been revealed of your life, I really believe that you did enjoy those hymns, and therefore believe that there is hope. Even those hymns may have been heard in Heaven, and be remembered there now to your good."

Incidentally the letter shows up its writer in a better light than heretofore, since at the time it was penned Brion was actively suffering on Peace's account, the neighbours all declaring that whilst they were associated he must have known something of the master criminal's doings.

In a reply to his partner's exhortation Peace was careful to summarily knock the idea on the head.

> "Now, Mr. Brion," he wrote in his characteristic fashion, "it will give me great pleasure to speak the truth in this matter. In the first place, I wish you to understand that whatever I have been in the course of my life in the shape of telling lies, I have done with all that for the remainder of my life, which will be ended on the 25th of this month. I do say truly that neither you nor any friend or neighbour within miles of Nunhead or Peckham Rye did know anything of what I was doing of, for I always represented myself as an independent man, and also was very careful about going out and coming in, so that I know there was no suspicion on me. As for you, Mr. Brion, you might have lived in my house along with me and I should not have let you know anything. So that I am very sorry to think that the people round Peckham Rye should so most wrongfully affect an innocent man's

character by connecting it with one of the worst men that this world ever produced."

Shortly after this correspondence the two met in the condemned cell at Armley.

On this occasion an attempt seems to have been made to induce the convict to disclose the names of the receivers with whom he had done business; but Peace stolidly refused to peach. He declared that these men had a perfect right to buy things that were offered to them for sale. As for the money they had handed over to him—well, he had "worked hard" for it.

A few days before the execution Peace wrote the following letter to Mr. Littlewood, the vicar of Darnall:—

"I hope you will preach my funeral sermon of advice to the people of Darnall on Sunday next, and tell them that my life has been a very bad, wicked, and base one, full of misery and imprisonment. I hope and trust they will take warning by my most miserable life and end. I hope and trust that they will have mercy and compassion upon every member of my family, and not insult them or cast slurs or remarks at them upon my account, for they cannot help anything that I have done. So, my dear friend, do have compassion upon them. Do not abuse them, but pity them. I ask this favour in my last moment when upon the scaffold a moment before I die. May God bless you all. I die in the full hope that the great God has heard my prayer and forgiven my wicked sins as freely as I forgive those who have sinned against me. Farewell. God bless you all."

He adopted a similar tone towards his family whenever they came to see him. Before his death he made a will in which he divided what he thought was left of his ill-gotten gains between Mrs. Hannah Peace, his brother Daniel, his daughter Mrs. Bolsover, and Willie Ward.

That last act of attempted justice done, he finally resigned himself to the fate which was awaiting him. He wrote as follows to his wife and family:—

"I tell you this great joy that I could not tell you yesterday—for I could not. No fear now, for it is all cleared up as to where I am going to. I am going to Heaven, or to the place that the good go to who die in the Lord, to the place appointed by my God for the good to wait until the resurrection of the dead. So do not forget our meeting-place is in Heaven. So do come at the last, and you will find me there. This letter is wrote twenty-five minutes before I go to die so I must now say 'Good-bye' to all. So good-bye—good-bye, and God bless you all, for I am going to Heaven.—CHARLES PEACE."

THE LIFE STORY OF CHARLES PEACE

Amongst other letters he wrote were several to his relatives. He desired these to be regarded as his last words from the scaffold, so that they might carry double weight when they were read. One of them to his brother was as follows:—

```
L P
―――              H M C P M    12-78
C 4                  "From Charles Peace, H. M. Prison,
                          Leeds, February 25-79.
```

"Dear Brother,—

"I write to you, hoping you will take this as a warning from the scaffold, as I intend it to be handed to my chaplain when upon the scaffold the moment before I die.

"I am sorry to say that I have been a very bad, base, and wicked man the whole course of my life. None but God and myself know the extent of my terrible deeds. And what has it all profited me now?

"Oh, let me beg of you in my last moments to give yourself to God and try and walk in the narrow path that leads to eternal life. And may the great God in His merciful goodness pardon all your sins, and may we all meet in the end at His right hand in glory.

"I have prayed to the great and all-powerful God to forgive me all my sins, as I freely forgive all who may have sinned against me.

"That these few lines may have the desired effect upon you is the dying prayer of—Your Brother."

He also wrote to Sue Thompson, the only member of his family circle, curiously enough, who was not allowed to visit him. At Peace's request, an order of admission to Armley Gaol was sent her, but it was countermanded for a reason that was never disclosed.

In his letter to Sue, Peace said:

"A woman of your education and ability must succeed. I hope you will be prosperous in this world. My poor, poor Sue. O do forgive me for the trouble and the blows I have given you. God bless both of us. I am yours—Charles Peace."

Peace Talks of the Dysons.

About a week after the trial Mr. Littlewood, the vicar of Darnall, was surprised to find amongst his morning's post the following letter:

"Dear Sir,—This is from that poor, miserable man, Charles Peace, now lying under sentence of death in prison. Dear sir, I have a great desire to see you as early as possible this week, if you don't think it too much trouble or think that I am so base and bad that it is not worth your while to see me. But, O sir, do come and see me at once, for I have a great message for you to bear to the people of Darnall, and I think you yourself will not reject coming to see me. You will have to bring this letter with you, and the governor will give you further instructions. Please write back and let me know by return of post.—Believe me to remain yours, CHARLES PEACE."

On receipt of this letter the vicar hurried off to Armley Gaol, where he found his old parishioner in a state of great excitement.

At first Peace's talk was all about the Dyson murder.

He declared that he simply fired at Mr. Dyson in order to frighten him. Having spoken on the subject for a while, he proceeded to talk about his past. But he abruptly turned the subject when the vicar quietly suggested that if he was able to melt down gold and silver ornaments he could hardly dispose so easily of fur coats and jackets.

"Now, Mr. Littlewood," he said at last, "I want you to listen to this. I was in Manchester in 1876. I was there to work some houses. I went to a place called Whalley Range. I had studied a house there which I thought I could do. I was respectably dressed, because I made a point of dressing respectably, as the police never think of suspecting anyone who appears in good clothes. In this way I have thrown the police off the scent many a time.

"On my way to the house that night I passed two policemen on the road. There were some grounds about the house, and my object was to get into those grounds in the dusk and wait a chance of getting into the house. I walked into the grounds through the gate, but before I was able to begin work I heard a step behind me. Looking back, I saw it was one of the policemen I had passed on the road. I doubled to elude him. For the moment I was successful, and, taking a favourable chance, I jumped the wall. As I was dropping down I almost fell into the arms of the second policeman, who must have been planted for me.

"This policeman—I do not know his name—made a grab at me. My blood was up, being annoyed that I had been discovered, so I told him, 'You stand back, or I will shoot you!' He did not step back, so I stepped back a few yards and fired wide at him, purposely to frighten him, so that I might get away.

"Now, sir, I want to tell you, and I want you to believe me when I say it, that I always made it a rule during the whole of my career never to take life if I could avoid it. But the policeman was as determined as myself. After I had fired wide at him I observed him seize his staff, which was in his pocket, and raise it as if about to strike me. I saw I had no time to lose if I wanted to get away at all. I then fired a second time. I had no intention of killing him. We had a scuffle together. I did not take as careful aim as I should have done, and the bullet, missing the arm, struck him in the breast, and he fell."

In such terms did Peace confess to the murder of Police-constable Cock at Whalley Range, a crime for which the man Habron, at that very moment languishing in penal servitude, came so near to losing his life.

Habron was afterwards released and given £800 compensation for the wrong he had suffered.

By way of explaining his callousness in going to the trial—a story that has already been told—Peace further said:

"Now, sir, some people will think I was a hardened wretch for allowing an innocent man to suffer for my crime. But what man would have done otherwise in my position? Could I have done otherwise, knowing as I did that I should certainly be hanged for the crime?"

As may be imagined, this confession provided sensation enough and to spare.

The news soon leaked out. Although the full text of the confession was not published till after the execution, the effect of it was known all over the kingdom.

CHAPTER XXIV.

The Execution.

And now the book is nearly closed.

This is the last night on earth for the man in the condemned cell.

Peace must die in the morning.

At half-past ten the murderer swallows his customary sleeping-draught, but at first it does not act. He does not want it to. Sleep! He has no use for it any more. Besides, he wants to think, to meditate on life's might-have-beens—for the last time. So he sits wrapped in thought till at last the insidious drug takes action.

And now sleep has come. Has it? In a second he finds himself wide awake as ever.

No, he cannot. He flings aside the coarse coverlet that does duty for a counterpane and asks for the Governor.

Presently Mr. Keene comes in, and the two remain closeted together till half-past one; then the Governor retires and knocks up the chaplain, who hurries to the condemned cell, only to find Peace too drowsy even for prayer. So the chaplain creeps out on tip-toe, leaving the doomed man asleep at last.

Away in Leeds the town clock toils mournfully through the hours It is bitterly cold. It is snowing.

* * * * * * *

Six o'clock.

Peace awakes with a start and looks about him.

A warder gives a message at the wicket, and in comes the chaplain, who remains with the doomed man for an hour. Then they bring in some breakfast—tea, toast, bacon, and eggs. Peace munches busily away, saying little. What is the use of saying anything now?

Without the prison a great crowd is assembling.

Whilst they wait the murderer within gives his last directions about his correspondence. Suddenly he recollects the morning's post.

He asks for his correspondence only to be told that at the time the mail is opened he will be lying a strangled corpse in the prison mortuary. Scarcely has he heard it ere there is a clanging and rattling of keys as the door opens and in comes a glum procession of officials. Amongst them is an elderly-looking gentleman. He might be a retired banker, but—he carries a pinioning strap. Peace knows who that is. He eyes the strap furtively. He has heard of it before. . . So that is what they do it with, eh?

And now the Governor is reading the death sentence, and the prisoner's body is handed over to the hangman for execution.

Everything is ready, and they walk slowly out to the dirge-like monotony of the chaplain's voice. Peace shudders. . . . They are burying him already.

This is the order of the procession:

The Chaplain, reading.
A Warder.   Peace.   A Warder.
Marwood.
Two Warders.
Two Warders.
Two Warders.

As Peace entered the prison-yard a cold north wind swept up and chilled him to the bone.

He was deadly pale, but he walked without faltering. It was his dearest wish that he should show no white feather when it came to the end. This wish at least was gratified. No one could gainsay him.

Pity that the ground was covered with ice, for several times the convict slipped as he went, which was bad, for the reporters were watching him, and they would think he was afraid. Yet they did not do so.

The procession now came into full view of the scaffold, which had been draped in black sacking and painted black for the occasion. The rope was swinging to and fro in the breeze.

Six steps had to be mounted before the drop was reached. Peace mounted them, reciting the while such answers to the chaplain's prayers as he could think of. Even a murderer could find comfort in religion—and on the scaffold.

And now he was standing on the brink of eternity.

On either side of him stood a white-faced warder ready to support him should his courage fail at the critical moment. Marwood had already taken in hand the white cap, when Peace turned and spoke to him.

"Stop a minute," he said quietly, with a nod of the head towards

THE LIFE STORY OF CHARLES PEACE

the chaplain, who was in the act of reading the last part of the burial service. "Don't put it on yet. I want to hear this read."

The executioner paused, Mr. Cookson read "Lord have mercy upon us," and the condemned man responded firmly and reverently, "Lord, have mercy upon me; Christ, have mercy upon me!"

When the chaplain had finished reading, Peace braced himself up and made his final speech. It stands unique amongst those delivered under like circumstances as being undoubtedly the most fitting one ever delivered by a dying man from the scaffold.

"Now, gentlemen, you reporters"—Peace's voice was strong and clear, so that there could have been no excuse for the four different Press representatives blundering over the words—"I wish you to notice a few words I am going to say. You know that my life has been a bad one, so that when you find I died in the fear of the Lord you will see what sustained me now. Gentlemen, tell my friends that, thank the Lord, I feel quite sure my sins are forgiven me, and that I can now die happy and ready to meet them in Heaven at the last. I want you to say 'Good-bye' to them for me. Say that my best thoughts, that my last wishes are for my dear wife and children. I hope that nothing will be said hereafter in the press to disgrace or distress them. Oh, my friends, God bless you all. Amen!"

As the doomed man came to an end the chaplain's voice was heard loudly crying, "In the midst of life we are in death."

Marwood at this moment drew on the white cap. While the executioner was adjusting the rope Peace again spoke.

"Take care," he said, "I have but little wind and it is too tight."

"No, no," replied Marwood, "It is all right. I won't hurt."

One of the warders said to Peace, "Are you ready?"

"Yes," replied the convict, "I am ready if you are." Then, his voice sinking into a lower key, he added, "though I could have done with a drink of water," after which he raised his voice and spoke loud again, "God bless you all!"

Marwood instantly sprang the lever and removed the string holding it in position. The chaplain cried out, "Lord Jesus, receive his soul!" The bolt was drawn, the drop fell, and Peace died without a struggle.

Such was the end of Charles Peace, the most notorious criminal of the nineteenth century, the man who, as Marwood, the executioner, afterwards admitted, died the best and bravest death he had ever witnessed on the scaffold.

May his soul rest in peace.

CONCLUSION.

Such was Charles Peace, the man who, but for that intangible something that warped his soul, might have been anything; the man who was a desperate criminal.

He is known to have committed two murders, and it is not impossible that he murdered and maimed on other occasions of which nothing will ever be known. Yet old ladies used to send valentines to him; tramps composed poetry in his honour, and, after his execution, a man actually committed suicide for grief at the loss of a "hero."

What was the meaning of it all? There is no doubt that Peace impressed himself on the popular mind more than any freebooter since the good old days of the Dick Turpins and the Jack Sheppards. Many a notorious criminal has preyed upon society since that bleak morning when the little man expiated his crimes upon the scaffold in Armley Gaol. But there are still old men up and down the country who remember Charles Peace, not as a burglar and a murderer, but as a romantic rogue—a "caution."

It must be remembered, of course, that the Criminal Investigation Department of Scotland Yard did not come into existence until his race was well-nigh run. Pitted against a man like Sir Melville Macnaghten, one of the present assistant commissioners, and perhaps the ablest detective that this country has ever produced, Peace might possibly have made a less brilliant show than he did do.

Nowadays such modern innovations as finger-prints, the camera, telegraph, and telephone, it has been suggested, would have made short work of him. Be this as it may, but do not let us forget that within recent years glaring murders and amazing robberies have taken place, the perpetrators of which are still at large.

What modern and lesser criminals could do, is it reasonable to suppose Peace would have failed to accomplish?

The truth is that no mechanical device, however ingenious, is of service in the detection of crime without highly-trained controlling brains at the back of it.

Peace succeeded, as he would succeed again, because not a policeman in the country was sufficiently well trained to take a hand with him.

Yet it is not as a criminal alone that Peace will be remembered.

In the golden era that is to come, in which men will be bred with the same care with which we raise prize-cattle today, Charles Peace will be recognised as a creature of intellect utterly lost to the State, all for the want of a "turn of a screw" in his construction.

A man who could carve, who could draw, who could invent a patent guitar, to say nothing of that great life-saving device, the fireman's smoke-helmet; who could do a hundred and one things which marked him out as a genius—a perverted genius, if you will—amongst a lot of dullards, was something more than a common burglar.

THE END.

www.ingramcontent.com/pod-product-compliance
Lightning Source LLC
Chambersburg PA
CBHW011951150426
43195CB00018B/2890